Ma...
Guardians of the Galaxy

◆———————————————————————◆

Based on the Screenplay by
James Gunn and Nicole Perlman

Produced by Kevin Feige, p.g.a.
Directed by James Gunn

Level 4

Retold by Karen Holmes

Series Editors: Andy Hopkins and Jocelyn Potter

Pearson Education Limited

KAO Two

KAO Park, Harlow,

Essex, CM17 9NA, England

and Associated Companies throughout the world.

ISBN: 978-1-2922-0628-8

This edition first published by Pearson Education Ltd 2018

1 3 5 7 9 10 8 6 4 2

Set in 9pt/14pt Xenois Slab Pro

Printed by Neografia, Slovakia

Published by Pearson Education Limited

For a complete list of the titles available in the Pearson English Readers series, visit
www.pearsonenglishreaders.com.
Alternatively, write to your local Pearson Education office or
to Pearson English Readers Marketing Department,
Pearson Education, KAO Two, KAO Park, Harlow, Essex, CM17 9NA

Contents

Who's Who?

Peter Quill

Peter Quill is a human from the planet Earth. He spent his early years with his mother, and didn't know his father. Later, he was kidnapped by a team of outlaws called the Ravagers. He likes to call himself Star-Lord.

Rocket

Rocket is an alien who looks like a raccoon. He was given his intelligence by alien scientists, but personality changes also led to wild behavior. He works as a criminal with his friend and partner, Groot, and has a high opinion of himself.

Groot

Groot is Rocket's tree-like best friend and partner in crime. He comes from the plant *Flora colossus*, which grows on the planet X. He is unable to say more than "I am Groot," but he has human-level intelligence.

Drax

Drax is also known as Drax the Destroyer. In this story he has been sent to the Kyln, where the Nova Corps keep their prisoners. Ronan the Accuser destroyed his home and family, and now Drax wants revenge.

Gamora

Gamora is one of the galaxy's greatest fighters. When she was a child, the warlord Thanos killed all her people, the Zen-Whoberis, and kidnapped her. He turned her into a killer and she now works for Ronan.

Nebula

Nebula was also kidnapped by Thanos when she was a child, and is also a trained killer. When she fought Gamora in training, she was unhappy that Gamora always won. She now works for Ronan, too.

Nova Corps

The Nova Corps are space soldiers and police for Nova lands everywhere. Their orders come from their leader, Nova Prime, on the planet Xandar. They fought the Kree for more than 1,000 years, until a peace agreement was signed.

Ronan the Accuser

Ronan, or Ronan the Accuser, is one of the most dangerous aliens in the galaxy. He is a crazy Kree fighter who enjoys killing. He hates Xandar because Xandarians killed his father, grandfather, and great-grandfather.

Yondu

Yondu Udonta is the leader of a group of Ravagers—space outlaws and thieves. He was born on the planet Centauri-IV, and has blue skin. He controls his killing arrow with sound waves, especially by whistling.

Introduction

"This Orb comes from a time before the galaxy began. Inside is a stone—an Infinity Stone—that holds unimaginable power. There are six of these stones, and they control the galaxy. They can only be used by aliens who have enormous power—and they can destroy planets if they touch the ground."

When Peter Quill, an outlaw from Earth, finds a mysterious orb, he thinks that he can sell it and become very rich. But he is not the only person who wants it. Soon he is being chased by a smart raccoon and his tree-man friend, and a scary female fighter. Peter's boss, the outlaw leader Yondu, is also looking for it. Worst of all, Ronan the Accuser, a Kree warlord, will not stop until *he* finds the Orb. He knows that, with the Orb's power, he can control the galaxy.

Can Peter escape from his enemies? Can he stop Ronan before Ronan destroys the planet Xandar? And can Peter talk a group of crazy aliens into helping him?

Guardians of the Galaxy was first shown in movie theaters around the world—including more than 4,000 theaters in the U.S.—in 2014. In the first weekend the film was seen in 42 countries and it made $160.7 million. It is one of the exciting movies about attractive, powerful heroes that Marvel Studios has become famous for. Other Marvel stories—for example, *The Avengers, Avengers: Age of Ultron, Thor*, and *Captain America: Civil War*—can also be read as Pearson English Readers.

Guardians of the Galaxy, with its fast action scenes, great music, and humor, was an immediate success and was one of the most popular movies of the year. As well as the hero Peter Quill, and the trained killer Gamora, it introduced a group of aliens—including Rocket, Groot, and Drax—who quickly became favorites with the public. A second movie, *Guardians of the Galaxy Vol.2*, came out in 2017 and you can read that story, too, as a Pearson English Reader. Many of the characters from the first movie reappear, with some new and very frightening aliens. A third movie is planned.

The story of *Guardians of the Galaxy* begins on Earth, but it soon moves into space and to other planets. Morag is a planet in the Andromeda Galaxy. Thousands of years ago it was covered by oceans, but every 300 years the sea level goes down and buildings reappear. One of those buildings protects the Orb.

Another planet in the Andromeda Galaxy, Xandar, is the home of the Xandarians but is also the capital of many other lands, with a very mixed population of 12 billion. These lands are defended by the Nova Corps, and their most dangerous prisoners are kept in the Kyln. The Kyln is a terrible place and almost all prisoners die there within three years.

Knowhere is a place inside a great skull, on the edge of the universe, from which bone and other parts of the brain have been mined. Without laws, or rules, it has become a safe place for outlaws.

Sanctuary is the home of Thanos, a powerful warlord who controls a distant area of space with a large army.

The action in this story also takes place in and around spaceships: Peter Quill's *Milano*; Ronan's Kree warship, the *Dark Aster*; the ship of Yondu and his Ravagers; the spaceships of the Sakaarans, who fight for the Kree, and the Nova Corps spaceships.

Step into space, and enjoy the trip!

A Death and a New Beginning

It was very cold on nine-year-old Peter Quill's last day on planet Earth.

He was sitting alone in the hall, listening to his favorite music tape, *Great Songs 1*. He could see members of his family around his mom's bed in the hospital room. Her sickness had lasted for a long time—but now it was much worse.

"Peter. Your mom wants to talk to you." Peter looked up and saw his grandfather.

"Let's get these things off." Grandfather removed Peter's headphones and put them and his cassette player in the small bag on Peter's back. "Come on, son. She needs to see you. But be patient with her. She's quite confused."

Grandfather led Peter into the room. His mother looked pale and weak and was surrounded by machines. One of her sisters was sitting next to her bed, crying.

Peter's mom smiled at him. She looked anxious when she saw a mark on his face. "Were you fighting with the other boys again? Peter?" she asked quietly.

"They were hurting a cat. They hit it with a stick!"

"You're just like your father," Mom whispered. She looked up toward the skies dreamily. "You even look like him. He was a good man. He was a messenger from the heavens ..."

Peter saw his grandfather exchange looks with Mom's doctor. It was a look that said, *She's confused*.

Grandfather reached out and shook her shoulder a little. "Meredith, have you got a present for Peter?" he asked.

Mom looked down. She seemed to recognize the package on the bed and gave it to her son. Peter held the package. He wasn't sure what to do with it.

"That's for you to open after"—Mom couldn't speak for a few seconds—"after I'm gone. Your grandfather will take good care of you until your daddy comes back for you."

Grandfather took the package and put it in Peter's bag.

Mom took a deep breath and held out her hand. "Take my hand, baby." Peter looked at his mom's hand, but he couldn't move.

"Take my hand, baby," Mom said again.

Peter wanted to take his mother's hand, he really did. But he couldn't. He could only stand there, tears filling his eyes.

"Peter, take my—" his mother started again. Then she suddenly fell back onto her pillows.

The doctor and nurses rushed to her and pushed Peter away. The machines around her bed made loud noises.

Peter shouted, "Mom! No! No!"

Quickly, Grandfather pulled Peter back into the hall. "You must be strong, Pete," he said. "Stay here. O.K.?" He ran back into the room.

From the hall, Peter heard the rest of his family begin to cry.

That's when Peter ran away. He didn't think about it. He just ran. No one stopped him. He ran out of the hospital and across the parking lot. He ran through the trees and out into a field. And when he couldn't run any farther, Peter fell to his knees and started to cry.

He was still crying when a bright light from the sky shone down on him. There was a loud noise above him. "Mom!" he screamed.

He looked up and saw a large spaceship. The ship hung in the air, above the boy. Then slowly, the light pulled Peter up, higher and higher, into the spaceship.

On Planet Morag, Twenty-Six Years Later

For centuries, the citizens of Morag had worked together to build a great planet. But at the height of its success, the planet went through a terrible change. Suddenly, there were violent storms. Ocean levels grew higher, and continents were covered in water. The planet was almost destroyed and everybody left. For many centuries, Morag was visited only by brave, water-breathing aliens.

But when Morag's oceans returned to their earlier levels, a different type of visitor started to arrive.

One visitor's spaceship landed on the edge of a rainy, windy city. The pilot got out, his face covered in a mask. He walked through the rain toward the ruins of the city of Morag Prime. At the main highway, he pulled out a hand-held computer and shook the water out of it. It showed how the streets of Morag Prime had looked before they were destroyed. A red light pointed a route through the ruins.

The visitor looked around. He put on his headphones, and began listening to his favorite music tape, *Great Songs 1,* for the millionth time. As he pulled off his mask, Peter Quill smiled.

The pilot got out, his face covered in a mask.

Small animals with long tails and sharp teeth tried to attack him. He kicked them away and continued walking. He sang loudly and happily to the song on his cassette player.

Peter was human, but it was twenty-six years since he had left Earth. He had seen a lot. He had seen a planet made of fire with a moon made of ice. He had seen an army of aliens attack an enormous space fish. He had had an exciting time since the outlaw spaceship had picked him up. Peter had worked his way up from the lowest job on the ship until he was second in command to the captain. He was happy and life was exciting. But in all those years, there was one thing that hadn't happened. He had never become rich. As he walked into the ruins of a big old church, he knew that was going to change.

The inside was dark, but Peter was carrying a light.

"There it is!" He looked up at the high ceiling and saw a silver-colored metal orb far above his head, surrounded by bars that shone with a powerful electric force.

This was it. This was what he had come for. He was going to sell it to the Broker, and the Broker would make him rich. What was it? Peter didn't know, and he didn't care. When he looked at the Orb, he saw his future.

"Let's get you down here," Peter said. He pulled a strong magnet out of his bag.

When he turned on his magnet, the Orb moved toward it. For a few seconds it pushed against the bars, but then it broke through and dropped onto the magnet.

Peter shouted happily as he turned off the magnet and picked up the Orb. He was so excited that he didn't hear two alien spaceships land outside the church. Suddenly, he noticed that he was not alone. He was surrounded by soldiers.

"Drop it!" said their commander, Korath. His men lifted their weapons.

"No problem!" Peter said. He dropped the Orb and put his hands in the air.

"Who are you?" Korath demanded.

"My name is Peter Quill."

"And why are you here?"

Peter held up his hands. "Hey, I'm just looking around!"

"How did you know about this?" asked Korath, pointing at the Orb.

"I don't know what that is!" explained Peter. "I search for anything that I can sell and make money from."

"We don't believe you," Korath said. "You look like a Ravager." The Ravagers were a criminal gang that worked in this part of the galaxy.

Korath spoke to his soldiers in the Sakaaran language. They moved forward and took Peter roughly by the arms.

"Move!" Korath ordered. "We're taking you back to our spaceship."

"What?" shouted Peter. This was not going well. "Why?"

"My lord, Ronan, might have some questions for you."

"Oh …" said Peter. He needed to stop them. "I have another name. Maybe you've heard that …"

"What is the name?"

"Move!" Korath ordered. "We're taking you back to our spaceship."

Peter looked straight into Korath's eyes. "I am …" The aliens waited patiently. "*Star-Lord!*"

Korath looked confused. "Who?"

That wasn't what Peter expected. "Star-Lord! *The* Star-Lord! The famous outlaw!"

Korath turned back to his soldiers. "What is he talking about?" The soldiers just shook their heads.

"Oh, forget it!" What did Peter have to do to get famous around the galaxy?

At least the soldiers had stopped watching him. Peter took his opportunity and moved into action. He fired a flame-thrower at the soldiers. As they screamed in surprise and pain, Peter took the Orb and ran.

Korath pulled out his gun and fired. The shot missed Peter and blew a hole in the church wall.

"Thanks for the quick exit," Peter shouted. He hit a button that turned his boots into rockets, and the rocket boots pushed him out through the hole.

He landed some distance from the church and looked back over his shoulder. *He'll never catch me*, Peter thought. He ran with the Orb.

"Get him!" screamed Korath.

There were five more Sakaaran soldiers between Peter and his spaceship, the *Milano*. They shouted and lifted their guns.

"I don't believe this!" Peter said. He ran toward the soldiers. How could he get out of this situation? Then he realized that the soldiers' uniforms were made of metal. He reached into his bag and pulled out the magnet, switched it on, and threw it in front of him.

Immediately, the five soldiers were pulled toward it. They dropped their weapons as their metal jackets stuck to the magnet.

I can't believe that worked! Peter thought to himself. He jumped over the pile of soldiers as they tried to stand up. Finally past them, he ran into his ship and started the engines.

But he wasn't free yet. One of the soldiers had turned off the magnet, and now they were preparing an enormous rocket.

The rocket came straight toward the *Milano*. Peter turned the spaceship and the rocket missed him. A second rocket hit the ship, but Peter managed to save the *Milano* and fly away.

"Later, losers!" shouted Peter.

He had escaped from an army of Sakaaran soldiers with the Orb, something of great value. That should make "Star-Lord the Outlaw" even more famous!

The *Milano* was moving toward the planet Xandar, where Peter had arranged to meet the Broker. Peter sat in his pilot's chair, dreaming of the money he would get for the Orb. He would be rich. With so much money, he could do anything …

On the television, a news reporter was speaking. "*Fighting has begun across the Kree lands. The Kree are angry about the peace agreement signed by their leader and Xandar's Nova Corps …*"

The news was interrupted by a call on the video screen.

"Quill," said Yondu, the blue-skinned alien who was commander of the Ravagers.

"Hi, Yondu," Peter said.

"I am here on Morag. The Orb isn't here but I can see some dead Sakaaran soldiers. Is that your work?"

"Yeah, I was in the neighborhood. I wanted to save you the trouble," Peter said.

"Where are you?" Yondu asked.

"You know, boss, I feel bad about this … but I'm not going to tell you."

Yondu's face showed his anger. "I agreed to get the Orb for the Broker. I worked hard to get that job. And now you're going to cheat me?"

"You made a few phone calls," Peter said calmly. "I don't call that hard work."

Yondu's blue face turned red. "We don't do this to each other. We're Ravagers. We work together!"

"Yeah, we work together to steal from everybody," Peter reminded him.

"Everybody … not *me!*" Yondu shouted back. "When we picked you up from Earth, my boys wanted to eat you. They had never tasted a human before. I stopped them! You are alive because of me!"

"Yeah, yeah. Later, Yondu," Peter said. He ended the call and Yondu's face disappeared from the screen.

Nobody was going to make Peter unhappy on such a good day. He started dreaming again about all that money.

Back on Morag, Yondu turned to his men. "I will pay forty thousand units to the man who catches Peter Quill. But I want him alive. Do you hear me? Alive."

One of his men wasn't happy. "I told you that kid was trouble when we picked him up. Why didn't we sell him to the man who wanted him?"

Yondu turned angrily and took the Ravager by the throat. "*You* are the one who is trouble. Don't you worry about Mr. Quill. When we get him back, I am going to kill him myself."

He turned and faced the other Ravagers. "Now we need to worry about who *else* wants that Orb."

Ronan the Accuser Prepares his Plans

In the blackness of space a Kree warship, the *Dark Aster*, brought fear to the galaxy.

People didn't fear it because of its soldiers and their weapons. They feared the *Dark Aster* because its commander was Ronan. Some knew him as "Ronan the Murderer"; others as "Ronan the Warlord." These names pleased him, but there was one name he especially liked: "Ronan the Accuser." The people of this galaxy were, Ronan said, guilty of a great crime: they were *weak*.

Ronan was a member of a powerful group of aliens who had been lords of the galaxy. He was very strong and very tall, much taller than the people around him. He was strong in body and mind.

Inside the spaceship, Ronan stood up from an enormous pod full of black liquid. He held his warhammer, the sign of his power, in his hand. One of his men pulled a prisoner into the room. He was an officer of the Nova Corps, the Xandar army.

Ronan hated the Nova Corps. *He* wanted to rule the galaxy and they were stopping him. And the Nova Corps protected the weak, which made Ronan angry.

"You are in my court now," Ronan said. "I make the rules."

"I obey the old laws of my people, the Kree," Ronan told the officer. "I punish people who do not obey those laws. I do not forgive your people for taking the life of my father, and his father, and his father before him. I cannot forget the thousand years of war between us."

The Xandarian looked up at the warlord. "You can't do this. There is a peace agreement now between Xandar and the Kree."

"The Kree leaders have no honor," shouted Ronan. "You Xandarians and your way of life are a disease in the galaxy. I will destroy you!"

"You will never rule Xandar!" the Nova Corps soldier said bravely. He looked into Ronan's eyes. "You have broken the laws of the galaxy. You have stolen, you have killed many people ..."

Ronan smiled at the officer. "You are very brave. But you are in my court now," Ronan said. "I make the rules."

With one strike of his hammer, Ronan silenced the prisoner. The soldier's blood ran across the floor.

As Ronan cleaned his weapon, a servant entered. "Korath has returned, my lord," he said. "But he doesn't have the Orb."

"Bring him here!" Ronan ordered angrily.

He listened to Korath's report.

"I did not get the Orb, my lord, " Korath said nervously. "It was taken by a thief—an outlaw. He calls himself Star-Lord."

"Star-Lord?" Ronan questioned.

"He thinks he is important," Korath said, with a laugh. "He has agreed to find the Orb for someone called the Broker. We can catch him at the Broker's shop on Xandar."

Ronan stared at Korath. "You know we need the Orb for the success of our plan, Korath? I promised to get the Orb for Thanos. Then he will destroy Xandar for me."

"Yes," Korath agreed. "But …"

"Lock him up!" Ronan commanded with a wave of his hand.

"No, my lord, please! No! Do not punish me!" Korath shouted, but several of Ronan's soldiers removed him from their lord's sight.

Ronan turned to his most trusted assistants, Nebula and Gamora, two highly trained soldiers from different alien worlds. They were known as the "daughters" of Thanos, because that terrible lord of the galaxy had kidnapped them when they were babies and taught them to be soldiers— and Thanos was the only person who Ronan served.

He looked at the two women and made a decision. "Nebula, go to

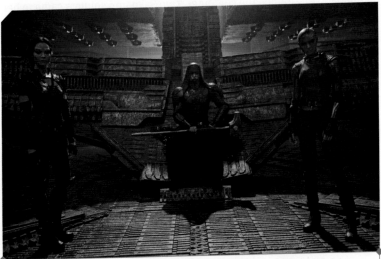

Ronan turned to his most trusted assistants, Nebula and Gamora.

Xandar and destroy this 'Star-Lord.' Get me that Orb," Ronan commanded.

"I am honored to do that," said Nebula.

"It will lead to your death," interrupted Gamora. "If you don't get the Orb, you will face our father without his prize."

Nebula looked at Gamora angrily. "I am a daughter of Thanos—just like you. I can do this easily!"

"That is what Korath thought, but this thief was better than him," Gamora said. "Why will it be different for you?"

Ronan watched with interest as the women argued.

"And who would go if I did not? You?" Nebula asked.

"I have been to Xandar many times and know it well," Gamora said.

Nebula shouted, "Ronan has already said that—"

"Do not speak for me," Ronan said, interrupting Nebula. He turned to look at Gamora. "You will not fail?" he asked.

"Have I ever failed?"

Gamora sat in the pilot's seat on the spaceship that would fly her to Xandar and programed the computer. Two Sakaaran soldiers came to her.

"We are happy to serve you, my lady," one of them said. "You are Ronan's most trusted servant. My brother and I look forward to success." He looked at the other Sakaaran.

"Yes," Gamora said. "But it is sad about the number of people we will lose."

The Sakaarans looked at her, confused. But before they could ask a question, Gamora took out her sword and killed them. She didn't want any of Ronan's men with her. She had her own plans.

The spaceship moved away with Gamora as its only living passenger. Looking out the window, she thought about the dangers. It would not be easy to fight Ronan.

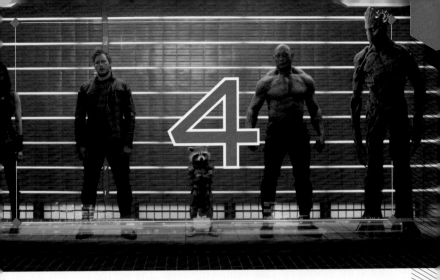

On Planet Xandar, Capital of the Nova Lands

It was a great day at the mall. The Xandarian sun was shining, the air was warm, and people were out having a good time. There were families playing, people in the stores, and friends eating outside the many restaurants. But Rocket wasn't enjoying himself.

Rocket was an alien a little over a meter tall who looked like an Earth raccoon. He was hiding behind some trees.

"Humans! All in a big hurry to get from something stupid to nothing at all." He pointed at an ordinary man and turned to his partner, Groot. "Look at this guy! They call us criminals but he's walking around with that ugly haircut! Now that *is* criminal! Isn't that right, Groot?"

But Groot, a tree alien more than two meters tall, wasn't listening. He was drinking from a faucet on the sidewalk.

"Don't drink that water! It's dirty!" Rocket shouted.

Groot quickly stepped away from the faucet and looked around innocently.

"I saw you," said Rocket. He looked at his computer screen. "Oh, there's one." Rocket's computer could recognize faces and he was looking for anyone who was wanted by the law—or who was wanted by anyone with enough money to pay him. The computer told him that this man was "Peter Quill, also known as the Star-Lord."

"O.K., let's see how much someone will pay for you."

Rocket checked the amount for Peter Quill on the computer. "Forty thousand units! So much money for a human? Hey, Groot, we're going to be rich!"

"I am Groot," said Groot.

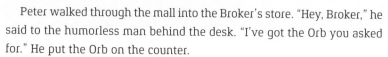

Peter walked through the mall into the Broker's store. "Hey, Broker," he said to the humorless man behind the desk. "I've got the Orb you asked for." He put the Orb on the counter.

The Broker looked at him carefully. He didn't really trust the young outlaw. "Hello, Mr. Quill," he said. "Where is Yondu?"

"He wanted to be here, sends his love … Do you have my money?"

The Broker looked from Peter to the Orb. "I guess I have."

"Hey, Broker. I've got the Orb you asked for."

"I almost doubled the price when I saw it. This is the best orb I've ever seen," said Peter. The Broker examined the Orb, then looked up at Peter. Peter smiled. "O.K. ... I don't know what it is," he said. "What is it?"

"I don't talk about my customers or their needs," said the Broker.

"Yeah, but that thing was hard to find. I almost died."

"In your type of work you can expect to get hurt," the Broker replied.

"Sometimes. But this was a crazy soldier working for a guy named Ronan," Peter continued.

The Broker stood up straight. "Ronan?"

"Yeah, have you heard of him? Who is he?"

The Broker shook with fear. "Ronan is a Kree madman. He is angry that the Kree are at peace with the Xandarians. He will not rest until we are destroyed. I don't want to make him angry."

"What about me? What about making me angry?"

"I am sorry, Mr. Quill, but I can't do business with you. Not if Ronan wants this," the Broker said. He put the Orb back into Peter's hands and pushed him out of the store.

"Wait ..." But Peter was too late. He was already out in the mall with the Broker's door closed in his face.

The Broker seems really scared, Peter thought. *Now what?*

A beautiful green-skinned woman was standing outside on the sidewalk. It was Gamora. "What happened?" she asked.

"I did a job for the guy in there, and he refused to buy from me. I hate dishonorable men. My name's Peter Quill—but you can call me Star-Lord."

Gamora walked toward him. "*You* look like an honorable man," she said.

"Oh, I can't say that," said Peter. "I *hear* it all the time, but I'd never say it."

He smiled as she moved closer to him. She really was very attractive. But suddenly the woman kicked him hard in the stomach, and took the Orb. She pushed Peter out of her way, and ran.

"Hey, wait, lady! That's mine!" Peter screamed. He chased after her. Gamora was fast, and she escaped easily.

This is so not good, thought Peter. Thinking fast, he pulled from his bag a piece of rope with a metal ball tied to each end. He threw the rope at her.

It was a good throw. The balls rushed past several surprised shoppers and fastened around Gamora's legs. She fell to the ground. Immediately, Peter was on top of her. He reached for the Orb, but Gamora easily broke the rope around her legs and kicked him off.

Peter fell backward and reached into his bag for his flame thrower, but Gamora attacked him again and he fell to the ground.

Rocket had watched all this. "Oh, no! She's going to hurt him! Don't let her hurt him!" he shouted, and he jumped on Gamora's back. At the same time, Groot put his branches around Peter to protect him.

"Put him in the sack and run!" Rocket shouted to Groot.

Him? Groot was confused by the word. Who was Rocket talking about? He looked at the sack, then at Peter, and then at Gamora. He jumped onto Gamora and tried to push her head into the sack.

Peter didn't know who the raccoon and the tree-man were. He only knew that he needed to escape. He took the Orb and prepared to run.

"Not *her*—*him*!" Rocket shouted at Groot.

Groot stepped back. Angrily, Gamora picked up Rocket and threw him at Peter.

"Aughhh!" shouted Rocket, as he hit the human. His body knocked the Orb out of Peter's hands, down to the lower level of the mall. Gamora jumped over the fence after it.

"No!" Peter screamed, and jumped onto her back.

Gamora pushed him to the ground. "Haven't you learned by now not to—"

"I don't learn," shouted Peter. "It's one of my problems!"

He pushed Gamora away and dived for the Orb. With it back in his hands, he turned to run again. But Rocket and Groot had followed him to the lower level of the mall. When he turned, he ran straight into Groot's sack.

"At last! Let's get out of here!" shouted Rocket. But Gamora stood in their path. "Are you joking, lady?" Rocket asked. "The human is ours!"

Gamora kicked Rocket away, then she turned her sword toward Groot and cut off both his arms. Groot screamed and dropped Peter.

Gamora quickly opened the sack to take back the Orb. But inside she found Peter looking up at her, a weapon in his hand. She stopped moving when he pointed it at her. He fired it and she fell.

Peter pulled himself out of the sack, ready to escape. That's when he realized that six Nova Corps spaceships were immediately above them.

A loud message came from one of the spaceships. "By order of the Nova Corps, you are our prisoners. You have put our citizens in danger and you have damaged property."

"Great, just great," said Rocket. He lifted his little raccoon's hands above his head.

Nova Prime, the leader of the Xandarian army, was talking to the leader of the Kree army over a video screen. "Ronan is destroying Xandarian soldiers across the galaxy," she said. "Surely the Kree must do something."

The Kree commander laughed. "We agreed to your peace. What more do you want?"

"We want the Kree government to stop him! He is killing children, families!"

"That is your problem. I have more important business." The Kree officer disappeared from her screen.

Later in the day, Officer Dey, a Xandarian soldier, reported to Nova Prime. "I have some good news. We have caught one of Ronan's officers, Gamora. The madman Thanos took her into his home when she was a child and trained her to fight. Recently Thanos lent Gamora and her sister Nebula to Ronan. We believe that Thanos and Ronan are working together." He showed her a picture of Gamora.

Then Dey pushed forward a picture of Rocket. "We took other prisoners at the same time. Some years ago, scientists worked on lower forms of life and gave them bigger brains. This is one of the things they produced. He looks like a raccoon, but he is very smart. And this tree-man is the animal's personal assistant." He showed Nova Prime a photo of Groot.

"The final picture is of Peter Jason Quill. He was taken from Earth at a young age by outlaws called the Ravagers. Their leader is Yondu Udonta."

Nova Prime looked at the pictures. "Put all the prisoners into the Kyln," she said. "We will question them there."

Inside the Kyln, the Worst Prison in the Galaxy

The Kyln was a cruel and frightening place with hundreds of guards. It held some of the most dangerous criminals in the galaxy.

"This is the worst prison in the galaxy," Rocket said, as the Nova Corps soldiers led him, Groot, Peter, and Gamora through its halls. "But I'm not going to be here long," he continued. "I've escaped from twenty-two prisons. This one is no different." He turned to Peter. "You're lucky that Gamora arrived. She stopped me and Groot collecting the money for you. Yondu and the Ravagers could be killing you now."

"A lot of people have tried to kill me over the years. A walking tree and a talking raccoon won't beat me," said Peter angrily.

"What's a raccoon?" asked Rocket. Was the word an insult?

"It's what you are," said Peter.

"There's nothing like me, except me," Rocket shouted.

Peter turned to Gamora. "What is that Orb? Why does everyone want it so much?"

"I have nothing to say to a thief with no honor," said Gamora.

"That's funny coming from you," Rocket interrupted. Gamora turned and looked angrily at him, but he continued. "I know who you are. *Everyone* knows who you are. You're Ronan's little friend."

"Yeah, we all know who you are!" Peter agreed. Then he turned and quietly whispered to Groot, "Who is she?"

"I am Groot," Groot whispered back.

"I know who *you* are. I'm asking who she is."

Rocket interrupted. "You won't get anything from him. He can't talk like me. He can only say 'I' and 'am' and 'Groot'. Those are his only three words."

"How do you understand him?"

Rocket shook his head. "I don't know. We just understand each other."

"I wasn't looking for the Orb for Ronan. I was going to sell it for myself," explained Gamora.

But she couldn't tell them any more because suddenly Peter saw one of the guards wearing his headphones and using his cassette player—the things that Peter loved most in the whole galaxy!

"Hey, those are mine!" Peter shouted. "Take those headphones off!" He rushed at the guard, but the guard picked up a stick and hit him in the stomach. "Those belong to me!" Peter screamed. He was still trying to fight. "And the cassette player. And the tape."

The guard hit him again. Then he walked away, listening to *Great Songs 1*.

The group was given yellow uniforms to wear, except for Groot. There wasn't a uniform big enough for a tree more than two meters tall!

They were taken into the main yard of the prison, where there were hundreds of noisy, screaming prisoners. In the middle of the yard was a tall tower from which the guards could watch them all.

When Peter and his friends arrived, the other prisoners started shouting at them. Some even threw things. A large rock and a couple of boots just missed Peter's head.

At first Peter thought the prisoners were trying to hit *him*. Then he realized that they wanted to attack Gamora. Everyone was aiming at her.

"We're coming for you, Gamora," they screamed. "You murderer! You're dead!"

Peter looked at Rocket, confused.

"They don't like her," Rocket explained. "A lot of the prisoners lost everything to Ronan's soldiers. She'll only last a day in here."

"But won't the guards protect her?" asked Peter.

Rocket laughed. "The guards are here to stop us escaping. They don't care what we do to each other."

Peter looked at Gamora. She had heard Rocket's words.

"It's O.K.," she told him, a sad look on her face. "Whatever pain my future holds, it is nothing compared to my past."

Before Peter could speak, a large alien came to him. "I am going to cover you in jelly and eat you!" he said.

Groot stretched out an arm, now regrown, put two fingers inside the alien's nose, and lifted him off the ground.

Rocket stepped into the middle of the yard and shouted until he got the other prisoners' attention. "Let's make one thing clear," he said. He pointed at Peter. "This human is ours to sell. If you want to get to him, you have to fight us first."

The prisoners heard the sound of bones breaking inside the large alien's nose. The alien screamed, and Groot threw him to the floor.

Peter looked around the yard, and pointed at Rocket and Groot. "I'm with them," he said.

But an enormous man with no hair on his head, no shirt on his back, and blood-red marks on his skin was watching Gamora. He knew her, and he had plans for her.

Rocket was right. That night, a group of men surrounded Gamora.

One of the prison guards gave them orders. "Take her down to the showers. It will be easier to clean up the blood down there."

Their voices woke Peter. When he went to the door, he saw a group of cruel-looking prisoners pulling Gamora away. She was kicking and fighting. Peter decided to follow.

"Quill? Where are you going, Quill?" asked Rocket.

Peter didn't reply. He was already moving away.

Rocket turned to Groot, who was asleep next to him. "Groot, Groot …
wake up, Mr. Sleepy Tree …" He shook his friend. "We need to follow Quill."

When Rocket couldn't wake Groot, he followed Peter alone.

The men took Gamora to a quiet part of the prison. One held a knife to
her throat. "We are going to kill you for your crimes against the galaxy."

Suddenly, they were interrupted by the enormous prisoner who was

"Ronan murdered my wife and daughter," Drax said angrily.

watching Gamora earlier. "Stop!" he shouted. "Do you know who I am?"

"You are Drax the Destroyer," the prisoner with the knife said nervously.

"Do you know why they call me that?"

"You have killed many of Ronan's men."

"That is because Ronan murdered my wife and daughter," Drax said angrily. He turned to Gamora. "He killed them where they were standing. And he *laughed*! On that day, I decided to destroy him. Because your lord, Ronan, took my family from me, I will now take *you* from *him*." He turned back to the prisoner who was holding Gamora. "Her life is not yours to take."

"Of course, Drax. Here." The prisoner handed Drax his knife.

But Gamora surprised them all. She moved quickly, took the knife, and pointed it at both Drax and the prisoner. "I, too, hate Ronan," she said. "And I hate my 'father,' Thanos. They are not my family. I have tried my whole life to escape from them. I am here because I finally have a chance of freedom."

Drax, too, moved fast, and he took the knife from her. "Your words mean nothing," he said. He put his hand around her throat.

"Hey!" someone shouted.

Gamora and Drax turned and saw Peter and Rocket watching them.

"Sorry, I didn't mean to interrupt," shouted Peter. "But I don't think you want to hurt her."

Drax looked surprised. "Do you know who I am?" he asked Peter.

"No, but you look very frightening," Peter said.

"I am Drax the Destroyer. No one in this prison gets in my way!"

Rocket was afraid. He didn't like this situation at all. "You heard the man," he said. He tried to pull Peter away.

But Peter shook Rocket off and continued talking to Drax. "This isn't the best way to destroy Ronan. You need to keep her alive. Don't do Ronan's work for him."

Drax looked confused. "Explain," he ordered.

"She's broken her promise to Ronan," Peter said. "And Ronan will want revenge. Keep her close to you. Then do you know what's going to happen?" Drax looked at Peter and waited. "Ronan will do anything to find her," Peter continued. "He will come straight to you. *Then* you can kill *him*."

Drax realized that Peter was right. He took his hand away from Gamora's throat and she fell to the floor. She was safe ... for now.

Drax looked at the knife in his hand. "I like this knife," he said. "I am going to keep it."

"But that's my favorite knife," the prisoner complained. Drax lifted his head and slowly looked at him. The prisoner held up his hands. "You keep it," he said quickly.

As they walked back to their prison room, Gamora spoke. "Thank you ..." she started. "I didn't expect that."

"Listen," Peter said. "I don't care if you live or die."

"Then why did you stop Drax?"

"Because you know where to sell my Orb."

Gamora shook her head angrily. Of course. This "Star-Lord" was just working for himself.

"I know where to sell it," she said. "But my knowledge is of no use here."

Peter pointed to Rocket. "He's escaped from twenty-two prisons."

"Yeah," agreed Rocket. He pushed Peter in the stomach. "We're escaping from here, too—and going straight to Yondu. He'll pay me and Groot for finding you."

"You said you had a buyer for the Orb," Peter said to Gamora. "How much will he pay you for it?"

"Four billion units," she replied calmly.

"Four bill—*what*?!" shouted a shocked Rocket.

"Seriously?" said an equally shocked Peter.

"Is that more than the money you will get from Yondu for Quill?" Gamora asked Rocket.

"Yes," said Rocket, still in shock.

"Good," Gamora continued. "That Orb is my chance to escape from Thanos and Ronan. If you free all of us, I will lead you to the buyer. We will share the money between the three of us."

A loud, unhappy noise came from behind them. They turned to Groot. He looked angry and upset.

Rocket laughed. "Asleep for the danger and awake for the money! That's Groot. We'll share the money between the *four* of us." He stared at Gamora.

6

A Smart Plan and a Great Escape

On the *Dark Aster*, one of Thanos's soldiers was talking to Ronan over the video screen. "Gamora has tricked you, Ronan!"

"We only know that she is a prisoner," Ronan replied. "She may still get the Orb."

"No. Information from the Kyln tells us that Gamora has her own plans for the Orb. Thanos wants to see you now. He is not happy with you."

Ronan traveled to Thanos's planet, Sanctuary, with Nebula. There, he was questioned by one of Thanos's guards. Thanos sat above him in an enormous chair, with his back turned.

Ronan spoke angrily. "Your daughter has caused these problems, Thanos. But you have called me here, to your planet!"

"Lower your voice, Accuser," the guard ordered.

Ronan didn't listen to him. "First Gamora lost a fight with a simple Earth-man. Then she was caught by the Nova Corps. She never wanted to work for us! She planned to escape and fight us!"

"Lower your voice!" the guard screamed again.

Angrily, Ronan lifted his warhammer and attacked the guard. The man fell to the ground, dead. Slowly, Thanos turned his chair around and faced Ronan.

"I only ask that you take this matter seriously," Ronan said to him.

"Oh, I do," Thanos said quietly. "But I don't take *you* seriously, boy. Your politics don't interest me. You have driven away my favorite daughter, Gamora."

Nebula, standing behind Ronan, looked angrily at her father.

Thanos continued. "I will continue to work with you, Ronan—*if* you bring me the Orb. But if you return without it, I will bathe the galaxy in your blood."

Nebula turned to Ronan. "This is one fight you won't win," she said. "Let's go to the Kyln."

In the prison, Rocket explained his escape plan.

"We need to get into that tower," he said, pointing at the guards' watchtower in the center of the prison. "And to get in there, I need three things. First, one of those."

Rocket pointed at a band on one of the guard's arms. The bands worked as keys, letting the guards in and out of the prison.

"Second, I need that guy's false leg," Rocket said. He pointed to a prisoner whose leg was made of metal.

"His leg?" asked Peter. "Are you serious?"

"Well, I certainly don't need the rest of him," said Rocket. "And last, do you see that black plastic cover up there? The one with the yellow lights?" He pointed at the wall, about six meters up from the ground. "There's a battery behind it—a purple box, with green wires. To get into the watchtower, I definitely need it."

Peter and Gamora looked at each other. "How do we get up there?" asked Peter. "Everyone will see us."

"I only have one plan to get out of here, and I need a battery for it!" Rocket repeated impatiently.

Rocket, Gamora, and Peter didn't notice Groot leave the table. The tree-man walked over to the wall and started to grow. Soon he was tall enough to reach the box. He started to pull out the battery that Rocket needed.

Rocket was still explaining. "Now this is very important. When that battery is pulled out, the whole prison will close down … So, we need to get that last."

As the battery came free from the tower, the lights across the whole of the Kyln went off. A second later, red emergency lighting came on. There was a loud, ringing noise.

Guards with weapons started to run into the yard. Guards in space pods flew toward the tower.

"What's happening?" Rocket looked up. He noticed Groot above them, waving the battery around and looking very pleased with himself. "Or we get the battery first and then think of another plan," he said slowly.

"Prisoner, put the battery down," shouted a Nova Guard.

Groot made a frightening noise as the guards in their space pods rushed toward him.

"Fire your weapons!" shouted one of the guards.

"I AM GROOT!!!" Groot screamed. He grew even larger and used his branches to protect himself.

When the Nova Guards fired their weapons, everyone went crazy. Prisoners started attacking guards. The guards tried to defend themselves.

"Well," said Gamora, looking at the fighting around them, "I will get one of those armbands."

"I'll get the leg," shouted Peter. He ran off through the crowd.

Drax saw a group of guards point their weapons at Groot. He stepped forward and started to fight. Bodies piled up around his feet. Taking one of the guard's weapons, he threw it to Rocket.

Rocket caught it. "Oh, yeah," he said, laughing loudly. This was fun. He began to shoot.

A group of guards ran toward Gamora. She fought them all and, one after another, they fell to the ground. She ran to the last guard and knocked him sideways. "I need the band on your arm," she shouted.

"Good luck! I'm not giving you that!" the guard laughed.

Gamora lifted up the guard by his arm. "Well, I will think of a way of taking it ..." she said in a scary voice.

Peter came running back to the others. He had the prisoner's false leg in his hand.

A Nova Corps guard tried to stop him. "Put down that—What is that, a leg? Put that down and move back into—"

But Peter didn't let him finish. He knocked the guard to the ground with the leg, then he picked up the guard's weapon. He turned quickly, and shot at a space pod that was coming toward him.

"You'll pay for hurting my partner," another guard said.

"No, he won't," said Drax, stepping out from behind the second guard. He killed both guards immediately.

Peter looked at Drax in surprise.

Drax said, "If you want your freedom, I am your friend. And Ronan's servant, Gamora, is not leaving without me."

"All prisoners—return to your sleeping areas!" shouted one of the guards.

The guard stopped when he saw Peter, Rocket, Groot, Drax, and Gamora walking toward him.

Rocket ran up Groot, like an Earth raccoon climbing an Earth tree. He stopped at Groot's shoulder. "You fool!" he screamed. He held onto Groot. "Take us to the tower! Now!"

"The animal is in control!" the guard shouted. "Shoot him."

Groot moved toward the tower.

At the same time, Gamora jumped across the hall to the top of the tower. She pulled Rocket up next to her.

Peter, still holding the false leg, also ran to the tower. He started climbing up Groot to reach the top.

Suddenly, a guard's space pod came toward him. It was going to shoot! But before it could hurt him, Drax appeared. He took the space pod in his hands and pulled it into pieces. Then he also climbed up Groot to the top of the tower.

Inside the tower, on the top floor, a guard was calling on the radio for help. "Send more guards—"

The guard stopped when he saw Peter, Rocket, Groot, Drax, and Gamora walking toward him. Groot picked up the guard and threw him out of the tower.

Gamora was shocked to see Drax. "What is he doing here?" she asked angrily.

"We promised that he could stay next to you until he killed your boss," Peter replied. He turned to Rocket. "Here's the leg you need," he said, throwing it to the raccoon.

"Great!" said Rocket. Then he dropped the leg out of the tower window.

"Wait! Don't we need that to escape?" asked Peter.

"No, we only need the armband and the battery. I was joking about the leg," Rocket laughed.

"What?!" Peter shouted.

"Silence! Let us hurry and escape this terrible place," said Drax.

"This is a mistake," Gamora said, looking at Drax with narrowed eyes. She didn't trust him. Drax stared back at her, but he said nothing. Gamora shook her head. She was going to die surrounded by the craziest fools in the galaxy.

Inside the tower, Rocket connected the battery to the computer's controls.

Peter looked out the window at the action in the prison yard. Prisoners were fighting guards. Guards were trying to take control again. There were fires burning in every corner.

"I don't mean to worry you, Rocket, but those are big weapons." He pointed down to a group of Nova Corps guards arriving with enormous rockets on their shoulders. The guards aimed the rockets up at the tower.

"I'm working, I'm working," Rocket said. He took two wires and tied them together.

The first of the Nova Corps's rockets hit the tower and some of its windows broke.

Drax was watching Rocket closely. Suddenly he spoke. "Oh, I remember animals like you. When we were children, we caught you and killed you. Then we cooked you over a fire. You were delicious!"

"That isn't helping!" Rocket shouted at Drax.

The whole tower shook as another of the Nova Corps's rockets crashed into it below their floor.

The guards aimed the rockets up at the tower.

"I've almost done it, almost done it …" Rocket said. The tower was still shaking.

"They're going to hit us again!" Peter shouted. The guards were preparing to shoot all their rockets at the same time.

"Get ready!" the guards' commander shouted. "Three … two—"

"Done!" shouted Rocket. He pushed the computer controls.

Slowly, the tower began to lift off the ground. At the same time, the guards began to fly into the air. They couldn't control their bodies—and they couldn't control their weapons!

"Rocket has turned off the gravity everywhere except inside this tower," Gamora explained, excited.

"Hold on," Rocket warned. He turned another switch.

The watchtower was built in pieces. Without gravity, its top floor started to lift away from the other floors. It was now free from the rest of the tower.

"Great, we're flying in the top floor of a tower. How does that help us?" Peter asked.

"Watch and learn, human," said Rocket. He was working on another group of controls.

The Nova Corps's space pods flew toward them. Rocket smiled. He used magnets to stick the pods to the outside walls of the tower. Then he used one of his controls to guide the pods. Their power pushed the tower in any direction he chose. Now the top floor of the tower had its own engine.

"I told you it was a good plan," Rocket smiled as he flew them out of the prison yard and through the gates. He was driving a big, square spaceship!

He guided their new spaceship to the place where the prisoners' clothes and bags were kept. Everyone went straight to Peter's things.

"It's here!" Peter shouted as he found the Orb in his bag.

"The Orb is here!" Gamora shouted. "Let's go."

"Wait!" Peter ordered.

He was searching in his bag for his cassette player and his headphones, but they—and *Great Songs 1*—weren't there. The guard hadn't returned them.

Peter handed his bag to Gamora. "Take this and go to my spaceship, the

Milano. It's the orange and blue one in the corner of the yard," he told her.

"Where are *you* going?" Gamora asked.

"Something of mine is still in the prison yard," said Peter.

"How do you expect to—?"

"Keep the *Milano* close to me. I'll meet you there. Go!"

Peter ran back toward the guards and prisoners fighting in the prison.

Gamora watched him go. This Earth-man was crazy. She led the others toward the *Milano*.

Peter pulled out his mask and his coat from his bag and put them on. Then he picked up his weapons.

When guards ran toward him, he shot at them. He didn't care how many he killed. Nobody was going to steal his music, a gift to him from his mother.

A team of Nova Corps guards waited at the prison door. They had orders to catch Rocket and his friends. The sight of Peter Quill coming toward them through the open door was a surprise!

And that surprise was all that Peter needed. With a gun in each hand, Peter shot the guards before they lifted their weapons. He ran past the fallen guards to the main office. The guard with the stolen cassette player was sitting at his desk with the headphones on and his eyes closed,

With a gun in each hand, Peter shot the guards before they lifted their weapons.

listening to Peter's favorite songs. The guy didn't know that a fight was happening in the yard. He was too busy enjoying *Great Songs 1*.

Peter lifted the Orb in the air and touched the guard on the shoulder. When the guard looked up, Peter crashed the Orb against his head.

"I told you that those were mine," he said to him. He pulled the headphones off the guard's head and the cassette player from his waist. Now Peter had to get back to his spaceship. The prison was full of guards. How could he escape? He looked out the office window and he thought of another way to his spaceship.

Gamora led Rocket, Groot, and Drax onto the *Milano* and Rocket started playing with the ship's controls.

"How will Peter get to us?" he asked Gamora.

"He didn't explain," Gamora replied.

"Well, forget this!" shouted Rocket. "Let's get out of here. You have the Orb, right?"

"Yes, it is here," said Gamora, opening Peter's bag. But there was no Orb.

Rocket jumped into the pilot's seat. "I'm not waiting here for a human with a death wish," he shouted. "We'll all be killed."

"We are not leaving without the Orb!" Gamora argued.

Rocket guided the spaceship out of the prison doors. Suddenly, he saw something that he never expected to see—Peter Quill, coming toward them using the rockets on his boots to walk through space!

They all watched in disbelief.

"This guy is crazy!" Rocket said. "That mask is no good for deep space."

Entering the ship, Peter pulled off the mask. His face was red as he greedily breathed in the air in the spaceship.

Drax touched him on the back proudly. "Flying through space without the correct equipment!" he said. "This man is brave. He will be useful in the fight against Ronan. Friend, what did you go back to the prison for?" Peter pulled the cassette player and headphones out of his jacket and showed them to Drax. "What are they? Some type of a ... a music player?"

"Yes," said Peter.

Drax's face changed. "You are crazy," he said angrily.

"Yes, he is," agreed Gamora.

"Maybe I am," Peter said. "But I also have this." He pulled the Orb from his jacket pocket.

"Great!" shouted Rocket.

For the next hour the *Milano* flew across space. Inside, Rocket was still examining the spaceship's controls. He started to pull pieces off them.

"Stop!" Peter shouted. "What are you doing? You can't destroy my spaceship without asking me first!"

"Can I use this?" Rocket asked, picking up the gift—still unopened—that Peter's mother gave him before she died.

"Don't touch that!" Peter said. He pointed at another piece of equipment on the floor. "What's that?"

"That's for when things get really dangerous!" Rocket smiled happily. "When we want to destroy moons!"

"We're not going to destroy any moons," Peter said angrily.

"You spoil all my fun!" Rocket complained.

Peter walked over to Gamora. "I need to know where your buyer for the Orb lives," he said.

"We are going in the right direction," Gamora replied.

"If we're going to work together, you need to trust me."

"And how much do *you* trust *me*?" Gamora asked.

"I'd trust you more if I knew what this is." Peter held up the Orb. "Because I think it's a type of weapon. I think we need to understand what's inside it."

"I don't know," Gamora said. "I am selling it to a collector who wants it. Whatever is inside it, he will keep it safe."

"Are you going to sell this Orb?" asked Drax. "I want to be a part of this plan."

Peter looked unhappy. Another one who wanted a share of the money! "What would you spend the money on," he asked Drax. "A shirt?"

"Why do I need a shirt?" asked Drax, confused.

"I thought you'd say that," Peter said.

"I will use my share of the money for my war on Ronan. What is the Orb's value?"

"Eighty thousand units," Peter said.

"Four billion units," Gamora said at the same time.

Rocket shouted angrily at Gamora. "What did you tell him the real value for? You ruined it!"

"I was taught to hurt people, not to lie to them," Gamora said.

"I will take an equal share," said Drax.

"O.K., we'll share it between the four of us," agreed Peter. Groot made a loud noise. "Sorry, I mean the five of us!"

Drax picked up the Orb. "If it is a weapon, we can use it against Ronan." He tried to open it—until Gamora pulled out her sword.

"Put it down, you fool!" she shouted. "You will destroy us all."

Drax moved toward her. Angrily, he lifted the Orb above his head. "Or I could just destroy you!" he screamed. "I let you live once—"

Peter quickly jumped between them. "O.K., everybody! Stay calm! Nobody is killing anybody on my spaceship. We're supposed to be partners! We'll stay together until we get the money." He turned to Gamora. "Partners?" he asked.

"We are working together—for now. We are not partners. I have never depended on anyone and I will not begin now. I will tell my contact that we are on our way. We will take the Orb to him." Gamora turned and walked away. "And Quill," she shouted over her shoulder, "your spaceship is very dirty!"

"I'm starting to really like her," Peter said.

Rocket looked at him, shocked. "You've got problems, Quill," he said. Then he also walked away.

Drax also looked shocked. "I will be in my bed," he said, and followed Rocket.

"That's *my* bed," said Peter. "*My* ship, *my* bedroom …"

It was too late. Drax was gone.

Now Peter was alone with Groot. "Just you and me, huh?"

This is a great group that I've found, he thought. *Just great.*

A Trip to Knowhere

Soon after the *Milano*'s escape, Ronan's ship—the *Dark Aster*—attacked the Kyln. The prison was already damaged from the fight between the guards and the prisoners and there weren't enough guards to stop Ronan's army. His forces broke through the walls. Soon the prison was under Ronan's control.

His men beat one of the prisoners. They wanted to know what he had learned about Quill, Gamora, and their friends.

"I don't know where they went!" the prisoner cried.

Across the room, Nebula held a knife to a guard's throat. "This one knows nothing," she said. "If he knew, he would tell us." She killed him.

Ronan marched through the prison. He had many memories of this place. When he was younger, the Nova Corps had brought him here for destroying a small planet.

Here he had met the Exolon. These strange aliens had taught him that "strength" was the only thing that was important; it was a crime not to use your strength. Here Ronan had discovered his life's dark purpose—to destroy the galaxy with his strength.

As he remembered those times, Nebula came to him. "The Nova Corps has sent spaceships to defend the prison. They will be here soon."

"And Gamora?" asked Ronan.

"She has gone," Nebula replied.

"Send my spaceships to every corner of the galaxy," commanded Ronan angrily. "Find the Orb—at any price. By any method."

"Yes, lord," Nebula said. "And ... this place?" she asked.

A guard screamed in pain.

"The Nova Corps must not learn about the Orb," said Ronan. "Destroy the Kyln. Leave nothing behind."

Yondu and his men were in the Broker's shop on the planet Xandar.

Yondu looked around and saw some small toys on the desk. "I like these," he said. He picked one of them up. "I collect them." He put it in his pocket and turned to the Broker.

"Now, tell me what this Orb is," Yondu demanded. "Why does everyone care about it so much? Then tell me who wants to buy it."

The Broker was shaking with fear, but he tried to be brave. "I can't tell you who my customers are."

Yondu walked toward him. He opened the front of his coat and showed his long, thin arrow. Slowly he began to whistle and, at the sound, the arrow flew into the air. "Now tell me," Yondu asked again, "who is your buyer?"

"Now tell me," Yondu asked again, "who is your buyer?"

On the *Milano*, Peter asked Gamora, "Where are we going? I need to program the computer."

"Knowhere," Gamora replied.

"Nowhere?" Wasn't the plan to find this big buyer of hers? The one who would pay so much for the Orb?

"No, not 'nowhere'," said Gamora. "Knowhere—with a *k*."

Half a day later, in deep space, in the middle of nowhere, they finally arrived at Knowhere. In all his travels, Peter had never seen a place like this. It was an enormous planet in the shape of a skull.

"Uh ... what is this?" he asked Gamora.

"It is the skull of an alien. It was cut from his body," Gamora reported. She made the words sound normal. She turned to Rocket. "Be careful, rat. There are no rules here."

"I hope its attacker isn't still here," Peter joked.

He drove the spaceship through one of the holes in the skull where there used to be eyes. Inside, Peter saw huts painted different colors built into the bone walls. Miners in single-person space pods were digging into the skull. They were taking out a thick, yellow liquid.

"Hundred of years ago, Tivan—one of the oldest beings in the galaxy— sent workers to mine the material that was left in the skull," explained Gamora. "This material can be sold for a lot of money. It is dangerous, illegal work. Only outlaws do it."

"Then I'll feel at home here," laughed Peter. "I live on a planet of outlaws."

They landed on Knowhere, and everyone climbed out of the *Milano*. It took longer than they expected to find Gamora's buyer because of Groot.

Children ran to them. "Do you have any units?" they asked. They were poor and thin and hungry. Groot felt sorry for them and grew flowers for them on his branches. This pleased the kids, but angered the other travelers. They wanted to do their business quickly—to sell the Orb and get away from this strange planet. Then they could share the money, and never see each other again.

"So, where is this buyer of yours?" Rocket asked Gamora.

"We must wait for his assistant," she replied.

Before she could say any more, Peter quickly pushed the others into a side street and looked back around the corner.

Yondu and a few of the other Ravagers were across the street. "Spread out," Yondu told his men. "Find Peter Quill. Remember, he calls himself 'Star-Lord.'"

Yondu hadn't had to hurt the Broker much before the Broker talked. He had told Yondu who wanted the Orb. He had also told the Ravager that this man lived on Knowhere. Yondu knew that Peter would go there if he wanted to sell it. Yondu just needed to sit and wait. Sooner or later the young man would come to him.

"Where did the Broker say that this buyer was?" Yondu asked his second in command.

"The Broker said the place was hidden," the other Ravager explained.

Peter dropped to the ground as Yondu and his Ravagers walked past the entrance to the street where he and his friends were hiding. After Yondu passed, Peter looked out. They were gone—for now. He relaxed and looked at his friends. They were staring at him.

"Is he a friend of yours?" asked Gamora.

"Not exactly," replied Peter.

Watching all the time for Ravagers, the others followed Gamora to a dirty old club. It was a loud, ugly, and smelly place. The people inside it were also loud, ugly, and smelly.

"Your buyer's in here?" asked Peter. Why would someone with enough money for the Orb come to a place like this?

"My buyer owns this place," Gamora explained.

They stepped inside.

Drax looked around. "What shall we do while we wait?"

"Oh," said Rocket with a smile, noticing a crowd on the other side of the room. "I'm sure we can think of something."

The entertainment was Orloni racing. Orloni, small animals like rats, had to race across the table to escape a small, hungry animal called a F'Saki. The last Orloni alive was the winner. Rocket loved Orloni races. Drax also thought they looked interesting.

On the other side of the room, Gamora and Peter sat at a table. "My contact is making us wait," Gamora complained.

"He doesn't want to appear anxious," said Peter. "It's the way we make a good sale. Your way is more: 'Fight, fight. . . do it my way!' "

Gamora smiled. "Thanos didn't teach me anything except fighting," she explained simply. "After he took my world and killed my parents in front of me, he turned me into a weapon. But when he said that he was going to destroy a whole planet for Ronan, I couldn't let him do that. My real parents taught me about a different kind of strength." She was quiet for a minute, then she continued. "Once, after Thanos kidnapped me, I asked, 'Why?' But there was no 'why.' The strong destroy the weak. That is how Thanos sees the galaxy."

Peter understood. "That guy that we were hiding from before—Yondu. When he took me from Earth, he taught me something, too. He taught me that nice guys get killed."

"So we both turned against the men who taught us," Gamora realized.

Peter shook his head sadly. "No," he said. "I didn't turn against Yondu ... I turned *into* him."

"And what is this?" Gamora asked, pointing at the cassette player at Peter's waist. "You went back for it. That was dangerous."

Peter showed it to her. "My mother gave it to me," he explained. "She loved to share her music with me when I was a child. I had the cassette player and a cassette with me when she ... when I left Earth."

Peter put the headphones over Gamora's ears and hit the "play" button. She put her head to one side and listened. "What ... what do you do with it?" she asked.

"Do? With music?" replied Peter. "Nothing. You listen to it. You dance to it. Dancing is the greatest thing in the galaxy."

"I am a fighter and I kill people," said Gamora. "I do not dance." She was talking loudly with the headphones over her ears. "But the music is good."

Peter slowly took her hands and pulled her toward him. They started dancing. His lips were very close to hers. He lowered his head and—

Suddenly Gamora's knife was pointing at his throat. "No!" she screamed. "I know who you are, Peter Quill. You can't trick me!"

They were interrupted by a sudden loud noise from the other side of the club. Rocket, Groot, and Drax were in the middle of a fight at the Orloni table.

"Oh, no!" Peter said.

They ran to help.

The Secret of the Orb

Near the Orloni table, Drax was holding Groot down on the floor and hitting the tree-man hard.

Rocket picked up his weapon and pointed it at the enormous man. He was ready to shoot when Peter and Gamora ran over and separated them.

"Stop! Stop! Stop! What are you doing?" asked Peter.

"This rat does not recognize that I am important!" Drax shouted.

"He keeps calling me 'rat,'" Rocket complained. He pointed his weapon at Drax again. "Everyone laughs at me!"

"No one is laughing at you," Peter interrupted.

But Rocket pushed Peter away. He pointed at Gamora. "*She* called me 'rat,' too!"

Gamora tried to apologize. "Rocket, I didn't want to make you feel bad."

Rocket waved his arms at Drax. "Let's see if you can laugh after I finish with you!"

Peter jumped between them. "Four billion units, Rocket! Just stay calm for one more night, and you'll be rich!"

That got Rocket's attention. "O.K. ... but when this adventure ends, I might shoot you all."

"You see?" Peter said. "This is why none of you have any real friends.

Five seconds after you meet somebody, you try to kill them."

Rocket calmed down, but Drax was still angry. "We have traveled halfway across the galaxy," he complained, "and I have had an argument with a wild animal. Ronan is still alive. I have not punished him for his crimes!"

He walked into a room at the back of the club, where a man was talking on the radio. He had an idea. Silently, he walked across the room and held his knife to the man's throat.

Back in the club, a secret door in one of the walls opened. A small female stepped out and spoke to Gamora. "Welcome, my lady. I am Carina. I am here to take you to my lord."

Gamora, Peter, Groot, and Rocket looked at each other. Finally, it was time to get their money.

They followed Carina through a narrow hall into an enormous room full of glass cases. The cases were filled with animals, plants, and other life forms. Some of them were very strange.

Carina explained. "We house the galaxy's largest collection of plants and animals. We also have examples of important pieces of art from the past." A man entered from the back of the room. "Let me introduce Taneleer Tivan. He is known as the Collector."

The Collector was a strange-looking man with white hair. He stepped forward. "Ah! My dear Gamora. Finally we meet." He kissed her hand.

Gamora wasn't in the mood to be pleasant. "Let's get to business," she said. "We have the thing we discussed."

But the Collector had noticed Groot. "Oh ... what is that thing there?" He walked toward the tree-man.

"I am Groot," Groot explained.

"A Groot! Wonderful," said the Collector. "Let me pay you now so I can own your body—from the minute of your death, of course."

"I am Groot," Groot said.

"He wants to turn you into a chair," Rocket said.

The Collector smiled and turned to him. "Is this the Groot's pet?"

"Its *what*?!?" shouted Rocket.

Gamora realized that soon there would be another fight. She interrupted.

"Tivan, we have traveled half-way around the galaxy with this Orb."

Peter took the Orb out of his bag.

"So, let us see what you have brought," said the Collector. He took the Orb and placed it on a table. He spent a few seconds examining it, then he smiled. "Yes … this is real."

"A real what?" asked Peter. "What exactly is this thing?"

The Collector didn't take his eyes off the Orb. "This Orb comes from a time before the galaxy began. Inside is a stone—an Infinity Stone—that holds unimaginable power. There are six of these stones, and they control the galaxy. They can only be used by aliens who have enormous power—and they can destroy planets if they touch the ground. Watch."

He switched on a video. The screen showed scenes of planets on fire across the galaxy. Slowly one of the planets broke into small pieces.

The Collector continued. "Once, for a short time, a group of six beings joined their hands together to use the energy of the stones. But in the end, the power inside the stones was too great for those six beings. It destroyed them." He was so excited that his hands shook. "It is beautiful, isn't it?"

With his back to the others, he used a special tool to open the Orb slightly so that he, and only he, could look inside. Still standing a short distance away, Carina watched him closely.

Rocket interrupted. "This is all very interesting, but we want to get paid."

"Of course," said the Collector. "How would you like to be paid?"

"In units, of course," Rocket replied.

The Collector opened a drawer in the table underneath the Orb. He didn't notice Carina walking slowly toward the Orb, her eyes fixed on it.

The Collector looked up. "Carina, stand back!" he shouted.

The girl rushed forward and reached for the Orb. "I will not be your servant any longer!" she shouted at Tivan. For years she had suffered at the hands of the Collector. He was a hard man, cruel to Carina and his other servants. She had heard the Collector talk about this Orb and its power, and she believed it would save her. If she could hold such power in her hands, she could free herself from him. But sadly for Carina, she didn't understand the nature of that power.

"Carina, no!" shouted the Collector … but it was too late.

When Carina tried to take the stone from the open Orb, her eyes grew large and turned black. Her face changed shape as energy from the stone filled her body. A bright white light came from inside her. She screamed and screamed.

Then there was a great explosion. Energy flew around the room, and within seconds there were flames everywhere. Everything started to burn.

Without a thought, Groot picked up Rocket and ran back down the hall. He wanted to get away from whatever was happening. At the same time, Gamora took Peter's arm and pulled him down to the ground behind a wall.

The explosion destroyed all the glass cases and everything the Collector owned. "My life's work!" the Collector cried. Seconds later, a piece of flying metal hit him and he fell to the floor.

When the explosion ended, Gamora and Peter pulled themselves up to their feet.

"I was a fool!" shouted Gamora. "Why did I think that Tivan could control what is inside the Orb? I didn't think about its power. I was too interested in my own plans."

She closed the Orb and picked it up. Then she and Peter ran down the hall and through the hidden door to join Groot and Rocket in the club.

"I can't believe you had that in your bag." Rocket told Peter.

"We must take this to the Nova Corps," Gamora said

"We must take this to the Nova Corps. Maybe they can control it," Gamora said.

Rocket's eyes were wide with shock. "Are you joking? We're criminals, we're wanted by the Nova Corps. Just give the Orb to Ronan!"

"Are you crazy?" Peter shouted. "He'll use its power to destroy the galaxy."

"So?" Rocket asked. "What's the galaxy ever done for you? Why do you want to save it?"

"Because I live there!" Peter said.

"Peter, listen to me," Gamora interrupted. "We cannot allow the stone to fall into Ronan's hands. We must go back to your spaceship and deliver it to the Nova officers!"

"O.K., I think you're right," Peter agreed. He paused. "Or we take it to someone who won't put us in prison. Someone really nice—with a lot of money."

"You have no honor!" Gamora said angrily. She walked away, holding the Orb. Peter and Rocket followed her.

They saw Drax in the street outside. His back was to them, his arms were stretched out, and he had a knife in each hand. He was laughing like a crazy man as he looked up at several of Ronan's spaceships. "At last, I shall meet my enemy and destroy him!" Drax shouted, as the ships started to land.

"You called Ronan?" asked Peter in disbelief. "He knows we're here?"

Then another spaceship landed, the doors opened, and Peter saw Yondu running toward him.

"Don't you move, boy!" Yondu shouted.

"Stand behind me!" Drax shouted to his friends, with a smile on his face. "In future years you can write about this in your story books. Your children and your grandchildren will enjoy it."

"I am Groot?" Groot asked.

"Yes, he is crazy," Rocket agreed.

"All brave men are crazy," Drax said.

This is the worst situation I've ever been in, Peter thought. *It can't get worse.*

Yondu and the other Ravagers were running straight for him. Gamora

"At last, I shall meet my enemy and destroy him!" Drax shouted, as the ships started to land.

moved quickly. Taking Peter's hand, she ran off with Rocket and Groot close behind her.

By this time, the Ravagers had seen the Orb in Gamora's hand. They ran past Drax, who was watching the open doors of Ronan's spaceships with expectation.

Gamora picked up a miner who was tying up his mining pod and threw him off a bridge onto the street below. Peter had seen these mining pods from the *Milano* when they first arrived on Knowhere. They were small, single-person spaceships with long arms on the front of them. These arms operated the mining tools that dug into the bone walls of the skull.

Gamora climbed into one mining pod, Peter into another, and Rocket into a third. Groot was too tall for a pod.

"Sorry," Rocket shouted. "We'll come back for you, big guy."

When Yondu and the Ravagers reached the pods, everyone was gone except the tree-man.

In front of Ronan's spaceships, Drax finally saw his enemy. "Ronan the Accuser!" he shouted.

Ronan went to him. "Are you the one who sent the message to me?" he asked. "Who are you? Where is Gamora?"

Peter had seen these mining pods from the *Milano* when they first arrived on Knowhere.

Drax was too angry to answer Ronan's questions. "You killed my wife!" he shouted. "You killed my daughter and destroyed my planet … Now you must fight me!"

"Is this a joke?" laughed Ronan. "I do not even know who you are."

Drax stood very straight. "I am Drax … the Destroyer!" he said proudly.

The conversation was interrupted by Nebula. "Gamora is escaping with the Orb!" she shouted to Ronan.

Ronan turned away and followed Nebula. "Get the Orb!" he told her. It was more important to find Gamora than to fight a stranger.

For Drax, this was a disaster.

Gamora, Rocket, and Peter were trying to escape but the mining pods were much slower than the spaceships of Ronan's Sakaaran soldiers.

The soldiers were receiving their orders from Nebula. "The Orb is in the space pod with Gamora. Shoot it down!"

To save Gamora and the Orb, Peter and Rocket had to destroy the soldiers' spaceships.

"Rocket," Peter shouted over the pod's radio. "We have to keep the Sakaaran ships away from Gamora. She must reach the *Milano*. She'll be safe there."

"How? These pods don't have any weapons," Rocket replied.

"No, but they are very strong machines," Peter said.

"Have you seen the size of the Sakaaran weapons? The rockets on their spaceships won't have a problem destroying us!" warned Rocket.

"That's not what I'm talking about," said Peter.

"What … Oh!" said Rocket, suddenly understanding. Quickly, he turned his mining pod and pointed it at one of the Sakaaran spaceships that was chasing Gamora. Then he increased his flying speed. The mining pod crashed into the spaceship's roof.

There was a big explosion and the Sakaaran ship started to burn. Rocket laughed—this was fun! He immediately turned toward a second Sakaaran spaceship, and flew into that one, too.

Peter flew his own pod over the top of another of the spaceships, then used the long arms on the front of his pod to pull the roof off the alien ship. He smiled down at the Sakaaran pilot. "Hi! Can I borrow your spaceship?"

The Sakaaran pilot was blown into space and Peter dropped his mining pod down into the spaceship. Inside, he used the pod's arms to work the spaceship's controls, and the spaceship's guns to shoot at other Sakaaran soldiers! One after another, the Sakaraan spaceships were destroyed.

Peter laughed happily. But then a message came from Gamora over the radio: "Quill! I can't escape! There are too many Sakaaran spaceships around me," she screamed.

Down on the ground, Drax wasn't going to let Ronan escape. When his enemy turned his back and walked away, Drax lifted his sword. He ran toward Ronan, ready to kill him. But just before Drax hit him, Ronan turned.

He took hold of Drax's sword, and threw it to one side. Then he took Drax by the throat, threw *him* to the ground, and walked away. Ronan was too powerful for Drax. To him, Drax was nothing more than an insect.

Pulling himself up, Drax made another run at Ronan. Ronan knocked him to the ground again. This time Drax didn't move. "You are a fool!" Ronan said. "I have destroyed many planets. I don't remember destroying yours. And I don't think I will remember destroying *you*."

At the same time, Peter and Rocket were chasing the Sakaaran spaceships in their mining pods. Another message came through from Gamora.

"Quill, I can't escape them! I will never reach the *Milano*," she said. "I have no choice. I am going into deep space. It is the only way that we can destroy the Orb!"

"What? Wait!" shouted Peter. "These mining pods can't fly in deep space!"

Nebula's spaceship arrived behind Gamora's mining pod. "You make me angry, sister," Nebula shouted over the radio. "Of all our brothers and sisters, I hated you least. When you took the Orb, I thought you were organizing an army. Now I find you hiding among thieves and murderers."

"Nebula," Gamora tried to explain, "if Ronan gets this Orb, he will kill us all!"

"Not all, sister," laughed Nebula. "You will already be dead." She fired a rocket and destroyed Gamora's mining pod. She watched calmly as it broke into pieces and Gamora's body fell out into empty space. The Orb hung in space, too, then a strong light pulled it up inside the *Dark Aster*.

Nebula called Ronan. "Brother, it is done," she said.

From inside his pod, Peter stared at Gamora's body. She was in deep space now, without enough air to breathe. She wouldn't live for long.

"Quill! Come on, we have to go before we die, too," Rocket said urgently from his pod. "We shouldn't be out here. There's no air and no gravity. There's nothing we can do for her." He turned his pod away.

Peter knew that Rocket was right, but he couldn't leave Gamora. Instead, he tried something else.

He turned on the mining pod radio. "Yondu, are you there? This is Quill!" said Peter. He hoped the Ravager could hear him. "I'm outside Knowhere. You'll find me at point 227-k32-8524. If you're near here, come and get me. I'm yours!"

"Quill! What are you doing?" shouted Rocket to Peter over the radio. "Whatever you do, don't—"

But Peter turned off the radio. He nervously put on his mask and fastened it to the life support system. This system would give him air to breathe when he was outside the pod.

Peter opened the door to his pod, and the air inside it rushed out into empty space. Then he jumped, using his rocket boots for power. He was aiming straight for Gamora.

Gamora's alien race was hard, their bodies strong, but even Gamora couldn't stay in deep space for very long. When Peter reached her, she was already dying.

"No," Peter shouted inside his mask. "Don't die!" He removed his mask and placed it over Gamora's face. Maybe he could give her a few life-saving breaths of air.

Already, he couldn't feel his hands and feet. He looked into Gamora's face. There were so many things that Peter wanted to do in this galaxy and so many things that he wanted to see. But, to his surprise, he wasn't sorry that he had tried to save Gamora.

And then, Peter's whole world disappeared in an explosion of bright white light.

Attack on the Dark Aster

The white light pulled Peter and Gamora toward a spaceship. Peter thought, *I'm supposed to walk into the light, aren't I?* But he couldn't walk; he couldn't even move. He fell asleep again.

When he awoke, he was still next to Gamora but now he was on the floor of Yondu's spaceship. Peter had had the right idea. Yondu had saved him so he could punish him!

Gamora was lying next to him. She coughed as she woke up. "Quill? How ... how did we get here?" she asked. "What happened?"

Peter held her face and looked into her eyes. "I don't know what I was thinking, but I couldn't let you die. I found something inside myself, something very brave—"

Gamora stopped him. "O.K.," she said impatiently. "Where is the Orb?"

"It's—well, Ronan and Nebula got the Orb."

"What?" Gamora shouted angrily.

A door opened. Yondu stood in front of them, surrounded by his men.

"Welcome home, Peter," he said.

Back on Knowhere, Groot held Drax in the leafy branches of his arms. A space pod crashed down next to them and Rocket climbed out. He stepped in front of Groot and examined Drax.

"You fool!" Rocket shouted at Drax as he woke up. "I'm surrounded by fools! Quill just let himself be caught by Yondu! And all of this happened because you tried to attack a whole army alone!"

Drax agreed. "You are right. I was a fool—an angry fool. I tried to be brave because I did not want to think about my lost family."

Groot looked at him sadly and put his hand on the big man's shoulder.

"Oh, boo-hoo. *I'm Drax and my wife and child are dead* ..." shouted Rocket. Groot covered his mouth, but Rocket continued. "I don't care if I sound cruel. Everybody's lost something. Everybody's seen terrible things. That's no reason for the rest of us to get hurt!"

He stood up and turned away. "Come on, Groot. Ronan has the stone now. We need to get to the other side of the galaxy as fast as we can. Then maybe, just maybe, we can live full lives before that crazy guy gets there. It's the only chance we have."

But Groot didn't follow Rocket. He called after him, "I am Groot!"

Rocket looked at him. "Save them? How? I know Peter and Gamora are the only friends we've ever had. But there's an army of Ravagers around them and only two of us!"

"Three," said Drax. "There are three of us."

Ronan had returned to his spaceship. He was standing in front of an enormous screen with Nebula and Korath when Thanos's face appeared. "I have the Orb," Ronan said. "I promised you I would get it."

"Yes, that was our plan," Thanos said.

"I bring you the Orb and you destroy Xandar for me." Ronan moved toward the screen. "But I have learned now of the power of the Infinity Stone inside the Orb. So why do I need you, Thanos?"

Slowly Ronan opened the Orb with his powerful hands and stared at the bright light from the Infinity Stone.

"My lord, you cannot do that!" Korath shouted. "Thanos is the most powerful person in the galaxy!"

Ronan held up the open Orb with one hand. "Not any more." He brought down his other hand onto the open Orb and light filled his body. Nebula and Korath watched the power of the Infinity Stone pour through him. Finally Korath offered Ronan the warhammer and Ronan put the stone inside it.

"You called me 'boy'!" Ronan screamed at Thanos. "I will burn the planet Xandar! I will destroy it! Then, Thanos, I am coming for you."

Thanos's face disappeared from the screen.

Nebula stepped forward. "After you destroy Xandar, are you really going to kill my 'father'?" she asked.

"You are very brave to question me!" Ronan replied angrily.

"If you kill him, I will help you destroy a thousand planets," Nebula promised.

"If you kill him, I will help you destroy a thousand planets," Nebula promised.

On the Ravager spaceship, Yondu hit Peter again hard in the stomach.

"Ow," Peter complained.

"Stop it!" shouted Gamora. Several strong Ravagers held her arms so she couldn't move. "Leave him alone!"

"After all that I have done for you, this is how you thank me?" Yondu asked Peter. "When I picked you up from Earth, my boys wanted to eat you! They had never eaten a human before. I stopped them. I saved your life!"

Peter stood up straight and looked into Yondu's eyes. "Oh, will you please be quiet? You've told me that story for the last twenty-six years. Normal people don't even *think* about eating someone else. They certainly don't expect that person to *thank* them for it!" He took a deep breath. "And you didn't save me. You kidnapped me. You stole me from my home and my family."

Yondu thought about this for a second, and then hit Peter again. Peter screamed with pain.

"You don't care about your home and your family," Yondu said. "You are scared because you are soft here." He pointed to his heart.

Gamora interrupted him. "Yondu, listen to me. Ronan has something called an Infinity Stone."

"I know what he has!" Yondu shouted.

"Then you know that we must get it back. He is going to use it to destroy Xandar," Gamora said. "Billions of people all over the galaxy will die."

"Who cares? It is not my problem," said Yondu. He turned to Peter. "Is this what she taught you? To care about other people?" He looked at the other Ravagers. "Let's teach Quill what happens when you work against us!"

Yondu pulled back his coat and whistled. His arrow flew out of his belt toward Peter's throat. "Sorry, boy, but a captain has to teach his men. This is what happens when you don't obey me."

Peter shouted, "Hurt me, and you'll miss the biggest fortune of your life."

Yondu laughed. "What fortune?" he asked.

"For the stone, of course," explained Peter.

"Not possible ... " Yondu said. "The stone is with Ronan on the *Dark Aster*. It is the most defended spaceship in the galaxy. No one can steal anything from Ronan. How would you—?"

"Gamora knows everything about Ronan, his spaceships and his army," Peter said. The arrow was still pointing at his throat but he tried to hide his fear. "What do you say, Yondu?" he asked, quietly. "You and me working together again, like in the old days."

"I lived on the *Dark Aster* for seven years," Gamora said. "It is weak in places. I am one of the few people in the galaxy who knows *where* it is weak."

Yondu thought about this. It would be satisfying to hurt Peter Quill ... But stealing from Ronan, from under his nose? Becoming rich at the same time? That would be even more satisfying. He laughed. "O.K., I agree," he said. "I'll work with you."

He whistled and the arrow returned to his belt. He shook hands with Peter, then threw his arm around him. "How do we start?" he asked.

But before Peter could answer, there was a loud noise—the sound of a shot near the Ravager spaceship. Then Rocket appeared on a video screen.

"Attention, fools!" he shouted at the Ravagers. "There is a madman on top of my ship with an enormous new weapon. I invented it, and I know what it can do. If you don't return our friends now, the madman's going to destroy your ship!"

Everyone on the Ravager spaceship ran to the window. It was true! Rocket was flying the *Milano*, and Drax was sitting on top of it. He was wearing a space suit and pointing a rocket at them.

"Send back our friends. I'll give you until the count of five," said Rocket.

"Only five?" asked Gamora.

Rocket immediately started counting. "Five ... four ..."

Peter ran to the video screen. "No, wait!" he screamed. "Rocket, it's me! We're O.K. Yondu and I have decided to work together."

Rocket's face and voice changed. "Oh, hi!" he said happily. "How are you, Quill?"

A short time later, they were all together in a room on Yondu's spaceship.

"What were you doing?" asked Peter.

"Saving you, of course," said Rocket. "That's what friends do."

"Saving us by shooting down Yondu's spaceship?"

"Drax was only going to shoot if they didn't give you to us," Rocket explained.

"But five seconds?" asked Peter. "How could they hand us back to you so quickly?"

"I am Groot," said a voice in the background.

"Yes," Rocket said to the tree-man. "They are very ungrateful." He turned back to Peter. "You can argue with the plan if you want. But it worked, didn't it?"

Gamora interrupted, "We need the Ravagers' army to help us save Xandar. So what are we going to do? Get the Orb from the *Dark Aster* and give it to Yondu? He will sell it to someone worse than Ronan!"

"We'll talk about that later," Peter said. "First we have to stop Ronan."

"How?" Rocket asked.

"I have a plan," Peter replied.

"*You* have a plan?" Rocket laughed.

"I have *part* of a plan," Peter said.

"How much of a plan?" Drax asked.

Gamora turned to Drax angrily. "*You* can't ask questions!" she said. "You are responsible for Ronan having the Orb!"

"How much of a plan have you got?" Rocket asked Peter.

"Less than a quarter," Peter said.

Rocket was shocked. "That's not a plan!"

Gamora interrupted. "That is only an idea."

Peter turned to her. "Now you're agreeing with *them*? I thought we were working together!"

"I am Groot," Groot said.

"Thank you, Groot," Peter said. "See? Groot understands. Guys, stop arguing! Yondu will be back here soon. He expects to hear our big plan. I need your help." He stopped for a second, then he continued. "Do you know what I see when I look at us? Losers." Drax looked angrily at him, but Peter continued. "I mean people who have lost important things. We all have. We've lost our homes, our families, our normal lives. Usually life takes away more than it gives to us, but not today. Today life has given us a chance."

"To do what?" Drax asked.

"To care about other people. To fight and not run away. I am not going to watch Ronan destroy billions of innocent lives."

"But Quill," Rocket said, "we can't stop Ronan. You're asking us to die!"

"I suppose I am," Peter said quietly.

Gamora spoke. "Quill, I have lived most of my life surrounded by my enemies. I am happy to die among my friends."

Drax stood up. "You are an honorable man, Quill. I will fight with you." Tears came to his eyes. "And when I die, I will see my wife and daughter again."

Groot also stood up. "I am Groot," he said.

They all turned and looked at Rocket. He shook his head. "O.K. I won't live for long." He stood up. "Are you happy now? We're all standing up—a group of fools standing in a circle."

Just then, some of the Ravagers came in. Gamora explained that the Infinity Stone could destroy all living things.

Peter said, "So Ronan has to put the stone on the ground on Xandar and all the plants, animals, people, Nova Corps soldiers—"

"*Everything* will die. Ronan must not reach Xandar," Gamora explained.

"Rocket will lead a team of Ravagers to blow a hole in the *Dark Aster*," Peter said. "Then our spaceship and Yondu's will enter."

"Won't there be hundreds of Sakaaran soldiers protecting Ronan?" one of the Ravagers asked.

"When they know we are on the *Dark Aster*, Ronan will hide behind great iron safety doors," Gamora said. "I can open the doors by turning off the power to them."

"Then I'll use Rocket's weapon to kill Ronan," Peter added.

Gamora brought out some small metal orbs and gave one to each of her friends. "When Ronan is dead, we can get the Infinity Stone. Put it into one of these orbs to contain its power. If you touch the stone, it will kill you."

"I'll contact one of the Nova Corps officers," Peter said. "I'll tell him that we're helping them."

Rocket was listening carefully. "O.K.," he said slowly. "There's one more thing we need to complete the plan. That guy's eye." He pointed to one of the Ravagers. The outlaw was tall and ugly, with long dark hair—and a large false eye.

The Ravager looked at him nervously.

"Seriously," Rocket said, but he couldn't stop laughing. "I need it! It's important to me."

Yondu's spaceship flew quickly through space until they heard a report that the *Dark Aster* was near them.

Yondu touched Peter's shoulder. "Remember, boy. At the end of all this, I get the Orb. If you try to trick me, we will kill you all."

When Officer Dey of the Nova Corps received a message from Peter Quill, he spoke to his boss, Nova Prime. "Quill says that Ronan has something called an Infinity Stone. And he is coming toward Xandar with it."

Nova Prime hid her fear. "Did this Ravager say why we should believe him?"

"He and his team escaped from the Kyln," Dey replied. "They are taking a great chance by coming here to help us."

"Do you believe this Ravager will help us?" Nova Prime asked.

Dey wasn't sure. He thought about it. Finally, he said slowly, "Yes, I do."

"Then order our people to leave the city before the attack begins," Nova Prime ordered.

As the *Dark Aster* flew toward Xandar, Nebula marched in to see Ronan. He was holding the warhammer containing the Infinity Stone on his knee. "Spaceships are coming toward us. They appear to be Ravagers."

Flying at top speed, hundreds of Ravager spaceships were coming closer and closer to Ronan's ship. Yondu's was at the front. "Fire your rockets!" Yondu screamed to his men. Balls of fire flew toward the *Dark Aster*.

Then the Ravager spaceships disappeared. "They are underneath us!" Nebula shouted to Ronan. "Go to your safe room and I will close the doors."

Hundreds of Sakaraan soldiers appeared to fight the Ravagers and the air was full of spaceships. The back of the *Dark Aster* was on fire.

Rocket was in one spaceship with the special weapon he had made. Peter, Gamora, Drax, and Groot were in the *Milano*. They were all following Yondu.

He was holding the warhammer containing the Infinity Stone on his knee.

Suddenly, a rocket from the *Dark Aster* hit Yondu's spaceship and he lost control. "I am going down," he said to Peter over the radio. "Don't play any more games with me, boy. I will see you at the end of this!"

Gamora looked at his ship as it disappeared toward Xandar. She radioed Rocket. "There are too many Sakaaran soldiers. We are not going to win."

But not all the spaceships around them were Sakaaran. Suddenly, a new voice joined the conversation. "Quill, this is Officer Saal of the Nova Corps. I didn't believe you would help us. Prove me wrong."

Hundreds of Nova Corps spaceships appeared and surrounded the *Dark Aster* as Peter flew the *Milano* inside the enemy ship.

A minute later, Nebula entered the safe room, deep inside the *Dark Aster*, to speak to Ronan. "Quill and his friends have broken into the spaceship," Nebula said.

"Continue toward Xandar," he ordered.

"But the Nova Corps has also arrived," Nebula said.

"They won't be important when we touch the ground on Xandar," Ronan said.

Down on Xandar, Nova Prime gave orders to the Nova Corps officers in their ships. "All spaceships—join together. Form a shield around the *Dark Aster* and block Ronan's route to the ground!"

Hundreds of Nova Corps pilots flew their spaceships close together until their wings touched. Slowly, they formed a shield around Ronan's spaceship. Now no one could get out.

Inside the *Dark Aster*, Peter, Gamora, Drax, and Groot stepped slowly from the *Milano*. It was very dark.

"I can't see anything," Drax complained.

Groot held up his hand and waved it. Hundreds of little stars came out of his fingers and flew into the air. They gave plenty of light.

Drax asked, "When did you learn to do that?"

"I think the answer will be, 'I am Groot,'" Peter said.

"The flight control room is this way," Gamora pointed.

Drax spoke. "I want you all to know that I am grateful to you. You forgave me for all my mistakes. It is good to have friends again. You, Quill, are my friend."

"Thanks," Peter said. He was more interested in the problems ahead of them.

"This stupid tree, he is my friend," Drax continued.

"Mmm," Groot said.

"And this green woman—"

Gamora turned to him. "Will you stop?" she demanded.

Just then, Nebula appeared in front of them. "Gamora," she shouted. "What have you done? You have always been weak. You stupid—"

Before she could say any more, Drax shot a rocket at her and she fell backward. "Nobody talks to my friends like that," he said.

Gamora looked at him, then she turned away. "Go to the control room. I will turn off the power to the safety doors so we can open them and find Ronan."

Peter, Drax, and Groot ran toward the control room. Gamora stayed behind and faced Nebula, who was still alive.

Slowly Nebula stood up. Gamora ran toward her. "Nebula, please—"
Nebula had nothing more to say. She began to fight.

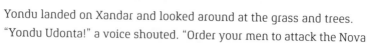

Yondu landed on Xandar and looked around at the grass and trees.

"Yondu Udonta!" a voice shouted. "Order your men to attack the Nova
Corps!"

Slowly Yondu turned around. He was surrounded by Sakaaran soldiers.
He opened his coat and gave a low whistle. His arrow came out of his belt
and went straight into the heart of the Sakaaran officer.

"Time to die," Yondu said, and smiled. He whistled again and the
weapon moved from soldier to soldier, killing them all. Then it flew at the
Sakaaran spaceship before returning to Yondu's belt. A few seconds later,
there was a great explosion and the spaceship was destroyed.

Nebula had nothing more to say. She began to fight.

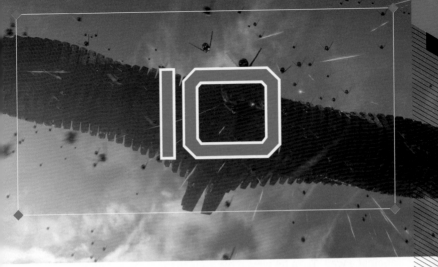

Can Xandar be saved?

Safe in his control room on the *Dark Aster*, Ronan said, "Enough of this. Prepare to attack Xandar."

Bombs began to drop on the planet from the Sakaaran spaceships that were still outside the *Dark Aster* and the shield of Nova Corps spaceships. The Xandarians who were still in the city looked up. They saw that death was coming and that it was too late to escape. From her watchtower, Nova Prime watched them. How could she save her people?

At the same time, Rocket and the Ravagers were flying down to Xandar. Rocket spoke over his radio to the Nova Corps captain, Officer Saal. "Keep Ronan up there. We'll take care of the people down here."

I can't believe I'm taking orders from a raccoon, Saal thought.

Rocket ordered the Ravager spaceship captains, "Shoot down the Sakaaran spaceships before they reach the ground."

Inside the *Dark Aster*, Peter, Gamora, Drax, and Groot turned a corner. In front of them was Peter's old enemy, Korath.

"Star-Lord," Korath said, laughing. "Finally I can fight you."

He and his men attacked, and the fight was bloody and violent. Drax had the strength of four men and hurt many of the Sakaaran soldiers but in the end even he lay on the ground, badly hurt.

"You will never get to Ronan," Korath told Peter.

But Drax wasn't beaten. He climbed to his feet and put his enormous hands around Korath's throat. Within seconds, Korath was dead. Drax continued to fight. Peter put on his mask and rocket boots and fought beside him.

More Sakaaran soldiers appeared. Groot put out one of his long arms and as the sharp branches ran through the soldiers' stomachs, they screamed in pain. Groot waved his arms to the left and hit the soldiers against a wall. Then he waved his arms to the right and hit them against the opposite wall. They screamed again, and Groot smiled.

Ronan stood near the safety doors. "Xandar!" he shouted. "Nothing can save you now!"

He lifted his arm and energy poured from the Infinity Stone inside the warhammer into the Nova Corps spaceships. One by one, they started to burn. Officer Saal's ship was the first to be destroyed. The shield around the *Dark Aster* was broken. Nothing could stop Ronan now.

Down on Xandar, Rocket and Nova Prime saw the explosion on Saal's spaceship. There was nothing they could do.

Rocket called Peter on his radio. "Quill, you have to hurry. We're being beaten down here."

"Gamora hasn't opened the doors yet," Peter said.

After a hard fight, Nebula lay on the floor of the *Dark Aster*. As Gamora reached for the switch that opened the safety doors so Peter could reach Ronan, Nebula stood up again. She attacked Gamora with her knife.

With the last of her strength, Gamora kicked Nebula.

Nebula flew backward, out of the spaceship's open door. Now she was hanging above deep space.

Gamora couldn't let her sister die. She reached a hand toward her and stopped her falling. "Nebula, sister. Help us fight Ronan. You know he is crazy."

Nebula looked into Gamora's eyes. "You are *both* crazy," she said. Then she cut through her own wrist and the rest of her body fell away into deep space.

Gamora thought that her sister was dead. But Nebula fell thousands of meters, and landed on top of a Ravager spaceship. She broke through the window.

"Get out!" she screamed at the pilot, and pushed him out of his seat.

Inside the *Dark Aster*, Gamora finally managed to open the safety doors. Peter, Drax, and Groot were next to her.

Ronan stood in front of them. Peter shot at him. There was a great explosion and Ronan fell down. Peter took off his mask.

"You did it!" Drax shouted.

But through the smoke, they saw Ronan slowly stand up again. He

Ronan stood in front of them. Peter shot at him.

turned toward them and lifted his warhammer. The energy from the Infinity Stone inside it threw them all backward.

Drax screamed with anger. He rushed toward Ronan, who calmly picked him up by the throat.

"I made a mistake," Ronan said. "I do remember your family. Their screams were like children's—"

Before he could say any more, a spaceship with Rocket at the controls flew in through the doors of the *Dark Aster*, destroying everything in front of it. Ronan disappeared into the flames and smoke.

But during the explosion, Rocket's spaceship was also destroyed—and Rocket was hurt. The little raccoon didn't move.

Peter carried him away from the pieces of his broken spaceship. The friends stood close together. Then Groot stretched out his arms and started to grow more branches to surround his friends and protect them from deep space beyond the open doors of the *Dark Aster*.

The *Dark Aster* was falling toward Xandar. Inside the spaceship there were fires everywhere, but Peter, Gamora, Drax, and Rocket were safe inside Groot's branches.

Slowly, Rocket opened his eyes. He was very weak but he realized what his friend was doing. Groot was using all his energy to save them. He was going to die.

"No, Groot," Rocket said, with tears in his eyes. "You can't do this."

Groot touched his face gently with a branch. "We. Are. Groot," he said slowly.

Then the *Dark Aster* hit Xandar and everything went black.

The sound of *Great Songs 1* played from Peter's tape. Drax started to move, then Gamora, then Peter. They were all lying on the ground somewhere on Xandar near the *Dark Aster*. All around them were fires, and pieces of the spaceship.

Rocket picked up a small branch. It was all that was left of Groot. "I called him a fool," he said. He was crying hard.

Ronan appeared through the smoke, moving slowly toward Rocket.

"You killed Groot," Rocket screamed. He ran at Ronan, but Ronan kicked him away.

Xandarians, including the Collector, stood around them.

"Look what your Guardians of the Galaxy have brought to you!" Ronan screamed at them. "Finally my father and his father will have their revenge on this planet. People of Xandar, the time has come for you to give up your old ways. I will save you." He lifted up his warhammer. He was ready to destroy their planet.

Suddenly, Peter started to sing. Ronan stopped speaking and stared at him. Then Peter began to dance in time with his song. "Listen to these words, man!" he said.

Ronan was confused. "What are you doing?" he asked.

"I'm dancing. Let's dance, brother." Peter laughed. "Me and you. We'll see who wins."

"What *are* you doing?" Ronan asked again. He was now very angry.

"I'm making you look at me," Peter said.

Behind Ronan, Drax lifted the weapon that Rocket had built. He shot it at the warhammer. The Infinity Stone flew out and Peter dived for it.

"No!" Gamora shouted. "Don't touch it!"

Peter fell to the ground, the stone burning his hand. He had to stop it touching the ground. But already the stone's power was too strong. Peter's skin began to burn.

In the distance, he heard Gamora cry, "Peter, take my hand." In his head he heard his mother, in her hospital bed, whispering, "Take my hand, baby." Why hadn't he taken it?

"Take my hand, Peter!" Gamora shouted again.

Peter reached out.

Then Rocket moved toward them and touched Peter's shoulder with his little hand. Finally, Drax's fingers stretched out and held Peter's shoulder. Now they were all side by side, touching, sharing the power of the Infinity Stone's energy.

"How can you do this?" Ronan shouted. "How can you hold the stone—especially you, Earth-man? Why aren't you all dead?"

"You said it yourself," Peter replied. "We are the Guardians of the

Galaxy." He opened his hand and energy passed from the Infinity Stone into Ronan's body. Ronan burned in the flames—and then there was an explosion and he disappeared.

Gamora put the Orb over the stone in Peter's hand. They had done it! They had destroyed Ronan!

"That was good," a voice said. "What a show!" Yondu was walking toward them with his Ravagers. "But we have business to complete," the outlaw said.

One of the Ravagers pointed his gun at Peter.

"You can't give the Orb to him," Gamora shouted.

Peter turned to Yondu. "Think again," he said. "I don't know who you're selling this to. But don't destroy the galaxy. Give it to the Nova Corps and let *them* control it."

"Give it to me, son." Yondu opened the front of his coat to show his arrow.

There was nothing that Peter could do. He gave the Orb to Yondu. The outlaw laughed and he and his men turned away.

"Yondu," Peter shouted after him. "Do not open the Orb. You know what's inside it. You know what it does to people."

Yondu laughed again and walked away.

As his spaceship left Xandar, Yondu turned to his second in command. "Quill is not a bad guy," he said.

"It is probably good that we didn't deliver him to his dad," the second in command said, "like we were paid to do."

"Yeah. His father was a fool."

Down on Xandar, the four friends watched Yondu fly away.

"He is going to be so angry," Peter said, "when he realizes that I gave him the wrong orb." He pulled the real Orb from his pocket.

Gamora laughed, but then her face grew serious. "He was going to kill you, Peter."

"I know. But he was the only family I had."

"You have a new family now," Gamora said.

Rocket was sitting on the ground, still crying. He held the small branch in his hand. Drax sat down next to him and touched the raccoon gently on the head.

Later that day, Yondu sat at the controls of his spaceship and looked at the Orb for a long time. He couldn't stop himself. He had to look inside. Slowly he opened it. Inside was a small toy—and nothing else.

Yondu started to laugh.

"Yondu," Peter shouted after him. "Do not open the Orb."

In the Nova Corps building, Peter was listening to Nova Prime.

"When we examined you," she said, "we discovered that you are only half-human. Your mother was from Earth but your father—he is something very old that we have never seen before. Maybe that is why you managed to hold the stone for so long." She turned to the others. "The Nova Corps wants to thank you all for saving Xandar. Please follow Officer Dey. He has something to show you."

As they walked across the room, Gamora turned to Drax. "Your wife and child will sleep easily now. You have had your revenge."

Drax thought about this. "Yes," he said. "But of course, Ronan was working for Thanos. It is Thanos that I need to kill!"

Officer Dey said, "We know that the *Milano* was destroyed in the explosion on the *Dark Aster*. We tried to keep it the same as your old spaceship, Quill." He pointed. There was a new orange and blue spaceship in front of them.

"It's just like the *Milano*!" Peter said. "Thank you."

"I have a family," Dey said. "They are alive because of you. You are no longer listed as a criminal. Please don't break any more laws in future."

Rocket stepped forward. "I have a question. If I see something I want—something that belongs to another person—can I take it?"

"That is a crime," Dey said. "We will put you in prison."

Drax asked, "And if someone upsets me, and I decide to remove his backbone?"

Dey looked worried. "That is murder. One of the worst crimes of all."

Peter interrupted. "Don't worry," he said. "I'll keep them under control."

"You?" Dey asked.

The young outlaw looked at his friends. "Yeah. Me."

In the next room, Nova Prime put the Orb in a safe box. Now it was under control and Xandar was safe.

That night, Peter finally opened the letter and gift that his mother had given him before she died. The letter said:

Peter, I know these last few months have been hard for you. But I'm going to a better place. And I will be O.K. And I will always be with you. You are the light of my life. My much-loved son. My little Star-Lord. Love, Mom

The gift was another tape of his mother's favorite music, named simply *Great Songs 2*. Tears filled his eyes. As he started to play the music, Gamora came closer to him and smiled. Slowly, she began to dance.

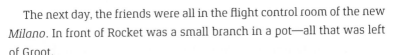

The next day, the friends were all in the flight control room of the new *Milano*. In front of Rocket was a small branch in a pot—all that was left of Groot.

"What shall we do next?" Peter said. "Something good? Something bad? A bit of both?"

Gamora smiled. "We will follow your lead, Star-Lord."

Peter laughed. "A bit of both." He turned to the controls and they rushed into deep space.

When nobody was looking, the little branch in the pot began to dance ...

"What shall we do next?" Peter said. "Something good? Something bad? A bit of both?"

Activities

Chapters 1-2

Before you read

1 Discuss these questions.

a Look at the pictures of the main characters at the start of this book. What do you know about them? Have you seen movies or read books about them? Which characters do you think are good, and which are bad?

b What type of book do you think this is: a love story, an adventure, a war film, or science fiction?

c Do you believe that there is life on other stars and planets in the galaxy? Give reasons for your opinions. What stories have you heard about aliens?

2 Look at the Word List at the back of the book. Check the meaning of unfamiliar words in your dictionary, then answer these questions.

a A *sword* is a *weapon*. List other types of weapons.

b Which words in the list are connected to space and space travel?

c Find four words for types of people.

d What *units* do you use in your country to measure or count: height/length?   weight?   distance?   money?

e Find two interesting facts about raccoons on the internet. Then share your information with other students.

While you read

3 Circle the correct answers to these questions.

a How old is Peter when his mother dies?
   seven   eight   nine

b What pulls Peter away from Earth?
   light   a magnet   gravity

c What covered and almost destroyed Morag?
   fire   aliens   water

d What protects the Orb?
  animals   bars   water
e What does Peter use to get the Orb?
  gravity   a magnet   his cassette player
f Who is the leader of the Ravagers?
  Korath   Yondu   Peter
g Where does the Broker live?
  Morag   Kree   Xandar
h What are the Ravagers?
  an army corps   outlaws   Sakaaran soldiers

After you read

4   Work with another student. Have this conversation between two Ravagers.

Student A: You are one of Yondu's men. Ask your boss about his feelings for Peter. Find out what Yondu plans to do next.
Student B: You are Yondu. Talk about your relationship with Peter. Explain why you are angry with him.

5   Discuss these questions.
  a Is Peter right or wrong to take the Orb?
  b Is there ever a good reason to steal something—or is stealing always wrong?

Chapters 3-4

Before you read

6   Look at the headings of Chapters 3 and 4 on the Contents page. Discuss these questions.
  a Ronan is the lord of the Sakaaran soldiers who attacked Peter. What do you think he plans to do next?
  b Peter now has the Orb. What do you think he will do with it next? Where will he travel and why?

While you read

7   Choose one of these words to describe the relationship between
    the characters.

    daughters   friends   assistants   enemies   sisters   servant   boss
    a Ronan and the Nova Corps are ....
    b Korath is Ronan's ....
    c Gamora and Nebula are Ronan's ....
    d They are ....
    e They are Thanos's ....
    f Rocket and Groot are ....
    g Nova Prime is Officer Dey's ....

After you read

8   Why does Ronan want to attack Xandar and the Nova Corps? Is
    there any excuse for his attitude and behavior? What do you think?

9   Explain in your own words:

    a why Ronan sends Gamora to Xandar.
    b why the Broker doesn't want to buy the Orb from Peter.
    c why Rocket wants to catch Peter.
    d why Nova Prime is afraid of Ronan.

10 You are a Nova Corps officer, writing notes for Nova Prime about
    the prisoners. What do you know about:

    a Peter Quill?   **b** Gamora?   **c** Rocket?   **d** Groot?

Chapters 5–6

Before you read

11 In Chapter 5, Peter asks, "What is that Orb? Why does everyone
    want it so much?" What do you think the Orb is, and why might
    it be important to the story?

12 Work in pairs. Choose a picture from Chapter 5 or 6. Describe
    what you can see. Discuss what is happening. What do you think
    is going to happen next?

While you read

13 Write the names. Who:

    a has already escaped from a lot of prisons? ....

    b do all the prisoners in the Kyln want to attack? ....

    c defends Peter when an alien wants to eat him? ....

    d has killed many of Ronan's men? ....

    e stops Drax killing Gamora? ....

    f knows where to sell the Orb? ....

14 Put these events in the correct order (1–10).

    a Rocket separates the top floor from the watchtower. ◯

    b Rocket makes a plan. ◯

    c The team escapes in the *Milano*. ◯

    d Peter and his team climb into the watchtower. ◯

    e The team finds the Orb. ◯

    f Prisoners and Nova Guards start fighting. ◯

    g Groot pulls the battery away from the wall. ◯

    h Peter returns to find his cassette player. ◯

    i The prison lights go out. ◯

    j Peter walks through space. ◯

After you read

15 Discuss these questions.

    a Why do Peter and Gamora give different values for the Orb, and why is Rocket angry with Gamora as a result?

    b Gamora thinks she is surrounded by the "craziest fools in the galaxy." Give two examples of crazy or foolish things that Peter and his team have done in these chapters.

Chapters 7-8

Before you read

16 What do you think is inside the Orb? What might happen if it is opened? Why does it have such great value? What do you think?

While you read

17 Draw lines between the correct parts of the sentences.

a Ronan orders Nebula   in the shape of an enormous skull.
b Knowhere is a planet   to watch the Orloni racing.
c Yondu arrives soon after   get into a fight at the Orloni table.
    Peter and his friends

d Rocket takes Drax   land on Knowhere.
e Gamora is interested   in Peter's cassette player.
f Rocket, Groot, and Drax   to destroy the Kyln.

18 Circle the correct words.

a The Collector wants to buy *Groot's / Rocket's* body.
b The Orb can *build / destroy* planets.
c Tivan *can / cannot* control what is inside the Orb.
d Drax has called *Yondu / Ronan* to the planet.
e Nebula orders the Sakaaran soldiers to *attack / save* Gamora.
f The Orb is pulled into the *Dark Aster* by a strong *light / magnet*.
g Peter saves *Gamora's / Rocket's* life.

After you read

19 Think about your answers to question 16. Were you right about
the Orb? What is it? How does it work? Who can control it? Who
do you think should own it?

20 Work with another student.

Student A: You are a travel broker helping a customer organize a
trip to Knowhere. Describe the planet. What will a visitor find there?
What will they see?

Student B: You are the customer. Ask questions about Knowhere.
Explain why you want to visit the place and what you hope to see
and do.

Chapters 9-10

Before you read

....

21 Discuss these questions.

   a At the end of the last chapter, Peter's world disappeared in an explosion of white light. What do you think will happen next to him and Gamora? What do you think the light is and where has it come from?

   b Before the end of this story, one of Peter's friends is going to die. Who will it be, do you think? How will they die?

While you read

....

22 Who is speaking? Who to?

   a "I couldn't let you die."

    ....   to   ....

   b "I know Peter and Gamora are the only friends we've ever had."

    ....   to   ....

   c "Why do I need you?"

    ....   to   ....

   d "I saved your life."

    ....   to   ....

   e "Do you know what I see when I look at us? Losers."

    ....   to   ....

   f "Everything will die. Ronan must not reach Xandar."

    ....   to   ....

   g "Do you believe this Ravager will help us?"

    ....   to   ....

   h "Time to die."

    ....   to   ....

23 What is the order of these events? Circle the correct words.

   a Rocket orders the Ravagers to shoot the Sakaaran spaceships *before / after* they reach the ground.

   b *Before / After* climbing to his feet, Drax kills Korath.

   c Groot smiles *before / after* killing the Sakaaran soldiers.

   d The shield around the *Dark Aster* is broken *before / after* Officer Saal's spaceship is destroyed.

e Nebula falls through space *before / after* landing on a Sakaaran spaceship.

f Rocket is hurt *before / after* he flies into the *Dark Aster*.

g Groot protects his friends *before / after* he dies.

h Yondu flies away in his spaceship *before / after* opening the Orb.

After you read

....

24 Discuss these questions with another student.

a Why is Gamora angry with Peter when he says, "I found something inside myself, something very brave—"

b Why is Rocket angry with Drax when he says, " I tried to be brave because I did not want to think about my lost family."

c Why is Peter angry with Yondu when he says, "I saved your life!"

d Why does Rocket laugh when Peter says, "I have a plan."

e Why does Rocket laugh after he asks for the Ravager's eye?

f Why does Nebula argue when Ronan says, "Continue towards Xandar."

g Why isn't Yondu afraid when he is surrounded by Sakaaran soldiers?

25 How has Peter's character changed from the start of the book when he first found the Orb? Is he now an honorable man? Give reasons for your answer.

26 Answer these questions in your own words.

a Why can Peter hold the Infinity Stone without it destroying him?

b Before he dies, Groot says: "We. Are. Groot." What does he mean? How do his words explain why he saved his friends?

c Why does Peter start to sing and dance in front of Ronan?

d What have you learned in this book about Peter's father?

27 Read again the part about the fight between Gamora and Nebula, then work with another student and have this conversation.

Student A: You are Gamora. Explain to Nebula that she is still your sister. Talk about your history with Thanos and Ronan. Explain how Nebula can help you and why you don't want her to die.

Student B: You are Nebula. Why won't you help Gamora? Why do you want Ronan to win? Explain how you feel about your sister and why you hate her so much.

Writing

28 You have been asked to write about this book for your local newspaper. Explain what type of book this is and describe the plot. Write about the characters: which ones are your favorites? What makes the book interesting and enjoyable? Would you advise other people to read it? Why (not)?

29 You are a guard in the Kyln prison. Your boss is very unhappy that Peter and his team have escaped. Write an email to him, explaining the events in the prison. Start at the time when Groot took the battery off the wall and all the lights went out.

30 You are a Nova Officer. Peter, Gamora, Rocket, Groot, and Drax have escaped from the Kyln. Write detailed descriptions of each of them so they can be found.

Name	
History/background	
Physical appearance	
Character	
Reason for being in the Kyln	
Action if you find him/her	

31 Imagine that you are making a *Great Songs* tape for yourself. Choose five of your favorite songs that you want to include. Explain what the song is about; when you first heard it; why it is important to you; how it makes you feel.

32 You work for a T.V. station and you are going to interview Rocket about his life and his time with Peter and the other Guardians of the Galaxy. Think about information that would be interesting to your viewers. Write a list of ten questions that you want to ask him.

33 You are a newspaper reporter. You witness the *Dark Aster* falling on Xandar and the end of Ronan. Describe the events in the correct order for your newspaper. Explain what you saw and what you thought was happening. Describe your feelings as the final fight took place between Ronan and Peter and his friends.

34 You are a movie producer and you are planning another *Guardians of the Galaxy* movie. Which characters will return? What dangers will they face? Who will they fight? Invent some new aliens. What do they look like? What do they want to do? Use your imagination!

35 You are Gamora. Write a letter to a friend, at the end of this story, telling her what you think about Peter Quill. What is your relationship with him? Do you like him? Why (not)? Do you want to continue flying through space with him? Why (not)?

36 Orloni races are a very popular sport on Knowhere. Write about the most popular sport in your country. Describe how the sport is played, and the most important rules. Who enjoys playing and watching this sport?

37 *Guardians of the Galaxy* is about space travel and aliens. What other science fiction movies or T.V. programs have you enjoyed? What were they about, and why did you like them? Write a report for a movie magazine.

Word List

alien (n) in stories, someone or something from another world

arrow (n) a thin, straight stick with a sharp point at one end, used as a weapon

battery (n) something that delivers a supply of electricity

broker (n) someone who buys and sells things for other people

corps (n) an army group with special duties (a medical corps, or corps of engineers, for example)

galaxy (n) a large group of stars

gravity (n) the force that keeps things on the ground

guardian (n) someone who protects or defends something

honor (n) strong beliefs about right and wrong. An *honorable* person always behaves well.

infinity (n) the state of being without limits (infinite space, for example)

lord (n) someone with an important place in society; a *warlord* leads an unofficial army

magnet (n) something that pulls toward it any metal with iron in it

mask (n) something that covers your face to protect it

mine (v) to dig something (gold, for example) out of a deep hole in the ground or the side of a mountain

orb (n) something in the shape of a ball. Sometimes kings and queens carry golden orbs.

outlaw (n) a criminal who is running away from the law

planet (n) a body in space that moves around the sun or another star

pod (n) a container, or a small space vehicle

raccoon (n) a small North American animal

revenge (n) punishment for someone who harmed you

rocket (n) a vehicle for traveling in space

screen (n) the part of a computer (or T.V.) where you see information or pictures

shield (n) something that you hold in front of your body to protect you from attacks

skull (n) the bones of a person's or animal's head

sword (n) a long flat piece of metal with a sharp point and a handle that is used for fighting

tower (n) a tall, narrow building

unit (n) an amount used as a measure of something

warhammer (n) a metal tool used to show power

weapon (n) something that you use to fight with

whistle (v) to make a sound by blowing through your lips or teeth